W9-BPQ-724

EDUCATIONAL FACILITIES WITH NEW MEDIA

Alan C. Green, Editor
M. C. Gassman
Wayne F. Koppes
Raymond D. Caravaty
David S. Haviland

The final report of an architectural research study conducted by the staff of the Center for Architectural Research, School of Architecture, Rensselaer Polytechnic Institute, Troy, New York, under the terms of a National Defense Education Act Title VIIB contract (OE-316-031) between Rensselaer and the United States Office of Education. This material has been printed by the Department of Audiovisual Instruction as a service to American education without the use of government funds.

Published by   DEPARTMENT OF AUDIOVISUAL INSTRUCTION
NATIONAL EDUCATION ASSOCIATION

In Collaboration With   CENTER FOR ARCHITECTURAL RESEARCH
RENSSELAER POLYTECHNIC INSTITUTE

Library of Congress Catalog Card No. 66-25154
Copyright 1966, Center for Architectural Research, Rensselaer Polytechnic Institute

INTRODUCTION

The content of this volume is the result of a two-year architectural research study supported by the U. S. Office of education through Title VII – Part B (Dissemination) of the National Defense Education Act and conducted by the Center for Architectural Research, Rensselaer Polytechnic Institute. The printing and dissemination has been undertaken as a service to the educational and architectural professions by the Department of Audio-Visual Instruction of the National Education Association and at no expense to the government.

This publication has one objective: to optimize the conditions for learning by providing physical environments most conducive to learning when media are employed in the educational process. Toward meeting this objective a body of material – data, design studies, planning premises, reactions, and conclusions – has been collected and organized to offer guidance in the programming and planning of appropriate educational facilities. Since a number of different types of persons are involved in providing the educational environment, this guidance is offered in three sections, each directed to somewhat different, but overlaping audiences.

The overall title is Educational Facilities With New Media. Within it, Report A – "A Guide for Policy Makers" is directed primarily to boards, administrators, planning committees, and institutional planners; Report B – "A Guide for the Design Professions" is for architects, planners, and design specialists, as well as planning committees; and Report C – "A Technical Guide" is intended for those concerned with details of design – architects, engineers, equipment and furniture suppliers, and media specialists. As a building project moves from early conception, to programming, to design, to construction and finally to occupancy, it is hoped that this report will offer appropriate guidance to those responsible at each step.

By way of introduction, several points of explanation will place this publication in the proper perspective:

1. The primary concern is with the creation of environment for learning — with the planning of space and the designing of educational facilities. More might be said about staff organization, curriculum, teachers, resources, and finances, but this is essentially an architectural research report, and these areas are considered only in terms of how they affect school planning.

2. In dealing with school planning, educational philosophies which serve as the basis for planning cannot be avoided. However, evaluations and judgments as to the relative merits of such philosophies have been avoided as being outside the province of study. Rather than "here is the way to educate and therefore provide these facilities," the approach has been "if you adopt this philosophy, these are the implications for facilities."

3. Learning media are only part of the current educational scene, and a look at facilities with learning media is not a comprehensive look at all educational facilities. However, there are occasions when examining one aspect of the total system in depth is valid. Emphasis is intentionally on learning media, and their implications for facilities.

Within this framework, this publication will have achieved its objective if it can serve as a useful guide to those many persons who assume responsibility at various stages in a building program.

Finally, we feel this volume is a good example of three-way cooperation among government, as represented by the U. S. Office of Education sponsoring the original study; higher education, represented by the Center for Architectural Research as the researchers: and professional organizations, represented by DAVI of the National Education Association as the disseminators of the finished report.

ALAN C. GREEN
Director
Center for Architectural Research
Rensselaer Polytechnic Institute

FOREWORD

In 1952 the Department of Audiovisual Instruction began a series of publications, Planning Schools for Use of Audio-Visual Materials, with a 62-page statement on classroom design. Since that time DAVI has published other important titles in this series and numerous articles on building facilities in its magazine, Audiovisual Instruction.

Today the need continues for current information relating building design to educational media, and we are proud to be associated with the Center for Architectural Research of Rensselaer Polytechnic Institute in publishing this work which has been done by the Center under the direction of Professor Alan C. Green.

The field of educational media, like the field of architecture, can maximize its contribution to society only through such interdisciplinary work as this. The idea of a technology is a total concept, a way of thinking about problems as well as a way of solving problems. It is a system of men and things that can best be conceived by a totality of contributions representing a variety of skills. This book represents an important effort in this direction.

ANNA L. HYER
Executive Secretary
Department of Audiovisual Instruction
National Education Association

CONTENTS

REPORT **A**

A GUIDE FOR POLICY MAKERS

Library of Congress Catalog Card No. 66-25154
Copyright 1966, Center for Architectural Research, Rensselaer Polytechnic Institute
Photos by Carl Howard and Rensselaer's Office of Institutional Research, except
page A-12, A-V Center, San Jose State College, and page A-34, John Shaver,
Architect, Salina, Kansas.

EDUCATIONAL FACILITIES WITH NEW MEDIA
REPORT A: A Guide for Policy Makers

The final report of an architectural research study conducted by the staff of the Center for Architectural Research, School of Architecture, Rensselaer Polytechnic Institute, Troy, New York, under the terms of contract number OE-316-031 between Rensselaer and the United States Office of Education.

Alan C. Green
M. C. Gassman
Wayne F. Koppes
Raymond D. Caravaty
David S. Haviland

CONTENTS

1 LEARNING MEDIA: AN OVERVIEW

*Education
is many
things*

Education today is many things—it is nongradedness and team teaching; it is modern math and programmed instruction; it is educational parks and schools—within—schools; it is computer—based scheduling and it is learning media.

*Learning
media
defined*

Learning media are devices or methods of varying sophistication which are utilized for organizing, presenting and storing information, and for encouraging appropriate learning responses. Media are systems of communication, or aids in the communicative process. Learning media, in the broadest sense, include the teacher, the book, and the chalkboard, as well as television, motion pictures and slides. This suggests that there can be two classifications,—conventional learning media and new learning media. This report is principally concerned with the latter.

*Several
concepts
of media*

There are several concepts of what constitutes learning media. "You can use (the term) to mean anything which is intermediary in getting across an idea, or you can use it as meaning anything which is intermediary in bringing the teacher to the student, and these are two different things."* 7

---

*The quotations scattered through the report result from three invitational seminars held by the project staff. A summary of "Three Meetings in May" together with the list of participants is included in the appendix. The sources of the quotations are keyed to that list.

*Here media
are all
these*

Not wishing to belabor definitions, but desiring only to establish scope, this report deals with media in all these ways insofar as they affect space. Naturally more emphasis is placed on the newer media.

*Historic
development
of media*

The rapid expansion and development of learning media has been a phenomenon of this century, and the second world war can be identified as the major impetus. During the war, films, film strips, slides and records were perfected for helping to train the required civilian and military personnel. To these were added the opaque and overhead projector, and further refinements in film projectors in the period following the war. The 1950's brought the major development of television for education and more recently we have seen the growing use of programmed instruction and electronic-based information retrieval and data processing systems.

*Maybe too
many things
to choose*

From the listing of current media, one conclusion is evident; the educator has many—maybe too many—alternatives available as he structures learning situation with media.

L E A R N I N G   M E D I A   — —   M A T E R I A L S   A N D   M E T H O D S

---

visual display

projected------8, 16, 35mm motion pictures
slides, 2"x2" to 3 1/4" x 4"
film strips
overhead transperencies
opaque materials
shadows of 3-D objects

non-projected--chalkboard surfaces
charts, illustrations, graphics
printed materials

audio presentation

recorded--records and tapes
telephone
broadcast radio
systems for sound distribution

three-dimensional

models, demonstrations, miniaturized materials

combined audio-video

sound motion pictures
sound slides
printed materials with recorded sound
kits of audio-video materials

television

broadcast and closed-circuit
live and recorded
reception by monitors, receivers, or projector

programmed instruction

visual display and texts
audio presentation
combined audio-video presentation

information systems

film-recorded
computer-based

---

*Media used
to increase
efficiency
and
effectiveness*

Media have been used in education for two purposes—to increase both the efficiency and effectiveness of education. The book increased efficiency by making information available to more people economically; the chalkboard made classroom instruction more effective; and the training developments of the World War were certainly geared to efficiency. The current boom in learning media, supported by federal, state, foundation, and industrial programs, continues to be directed to increasing efficiency and effectiveness.

*Media has
always affected
school
design....*

The use of learning media in the educational process has always had an effect on the design of school buildings. The introduction of chalkboards into a classroom required appropriate viewing conditions and lighting; planning was often done carelessly and often not consciously, and the results were many inferior classrooms. The advent of slides and films required that a screen be introduced into the room, that a projector be positioned and powered, and that natural light be controlled by drapes or blinds. At that stage the use of projected media was a periodic event and the provision of one or two special rooms in a school—the audio visual room—was a relatively satisfactory solution for such infrequent uses.

*...but now to a
greater degree*

Learning media are now far more a part of the fabric of education, and may be employed everytime a class meets. With their increased use, and the expanded range and sophistication of methods, the concerns that media impose on educational facilities are far more extensive and significant than ever before. In fact, as this report emphasizes, the optimum utilization of learning media requires conscious planning efforts and the development of new design concepts in educational facilities.

*To understand
facilities, we
must first
review
educational
climate*

To understand the nature of the facilities required for appropriate utilization of media requires that we first explore the contemporary educational climate—its problems and directions—and the responses being made in the form of innovations in educational techniques, organization, and methods. As learning media are part of these innovations, such a review will spell out their current role, and will identify their implications for facilities and architectural programming.

2 CONTEMPORARY EDUCATION: CONCERNS AND DIRECTIONS

*Education can
be characterized
very differently*

American education today is characterized in very different terms, depending on the individual being questioned and his background. For some it is a period of excitement and dramatic change, while for others it is a period of disenchantment with the past and pessimism regarding the future. Some persons see little evidence of educational development in proportion to other areas of society, while others are concerned by the swiftness and magnitude of change in education.

*Generally, a
lack of
consistency*

American education is, in fact, characterized by a lack of consistency. There is change, but the quality, magnitude, and direction of the change vary a great deal from region to region, from district to district, and from school to school. Financial support, breadth of opportunities and quality of program also vary widely; in some places, change is a mere ripple, while in others it is a great wave.

*Forces
exerted on
education*

However, there are some forces being exerted on each part of the educational system. The magnitude and direction of the forces vary, but always the origins are in one or a combination of concerns which face, or need to be faced by every board, administrator, teacher and taxpayer in the country. These concerns can be identified in terms of NUMBERS, KNOWLEDGE, SOCIETY, and MONEY.

First Concern: NUMBERS

*More persons
now, and...*

- With an increasing population there are more students to attend our schools and colleges than ever before, and more significantly, a larger percentage of this population is attending school than before. Not only are there more children, but more persons of all ages are continuing through higher education and beyond. The future indicates still greater numbers.

*...in the
future*

"If we try to look ahead 10 or 15 years, considering the present acceleration of change in education, it seems clear that by 1970 or 1975, people will have accepted the idea of a continuous school, not only in terms of a nongraded school, but a school that runs all year round, the way a post office or a supermarket does. They will not go through school—they'll go to school. They'll start earlier and will finish later. They'll go whenever they're ready, and they will have guidance available that fits their age and stage of development."3

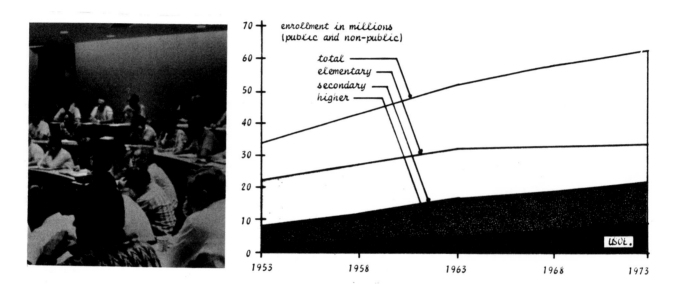

enrollment in millions
(public and non-public)

total
elementary
secondary
higher

70
60
50
40
30
20
10
0

1953   1958   1963   1968   1973

USOE.

Lack of teachers

• Classroom teachers seem to be in short supply (although there is debate on this point) and highly experienced, highly qualified teachers are rare (there is no debate on this). The supply of good teachers has not kept up with the demands for their services, and the rewards to the teaching profession have not been commensurate with its significance in society.

Shortage of buildings

• The construction of school buildings has not kept pace with the demands for additional space, not to mention keeping up with the need for replacement of obsolete facilities. Our more stable urban centers generally have sufficient schools, but of poor quality. Our suburban, fast—growing areas are simply short of school buildings of any type.

Size of the educational industry

• It's been noted that education is fast becoming the country's "largest industry." With bigness come not only opportunities for greatness, but also opportunities for ineptness, sluggishness, and resistance to change.

Second Concern: KNOWLEDGE

More knowledge accumulating faster

- We know more about more things today than we ever knew before, and we are accumulating this knowledge at a far faster rate than we ever have in the past.

Specialization of knowledge

- With such a body of knowledge accumulating at such a rapid rate, no one can be universally educated. Generally, to find one's role in life requires accumulation of specialized knowledge in one particular area.

Third Concern: SOCIETY

Education for survival

- Education is becoming associated with national survival— social and cultural as well as physical. Where once people were passive about education, they are now alert to its role in society. Or to put it another way, "The school is the institution in which democracy has the best chance of becoming conscious of itself. The fundamental problem is one of developing the kind of institution that combines the degree of individual freedom and initiative which is necessary for progress, with the degree of social cohesion that is necessary for survival."[1] *Sounds like an excuse also Galbraithes warnings*

World-wide Influences

- Educational concerns are no longer confined to the community or even to the nation. Education is one means being employed to assert the world's undeveloped and developing areas. In fact, after freedom, it is the primary need of society in the contemporary world.

Effects of automation and technology

- The talents of many men are in competition with the capabilities of new machines and the techniques of automation. A man's skills, his training and education, and hence his livelihood, may become obsolete during his lifetime. Society demands that education provide job training as well as a means of fulfillment during expanded leisure.

Education for self-fulfillment

- "I predict that within the next 25 to 50 years maybe 20% of the people are going to be able to do all the work that's needed, which means we'll have on the one hand this rapid explosion of knowledge, and on the other hand, the elimination of a lot of work. So I think that we are going to have to develop a non-work ethic to replace the old notion that work is good and everybody ought to do it; and in its place come up with the notion that self-fulfillment is good."[10]

Mobility of society

- Where quality and character of education was once a local matter, populations are now too fluid and too mobile to permit inequities in educational opportunities. A child may spend his fifth grade in the northeast, his sixth in the west, and seventh grade in the south; he should not be handicapped by this movement. Further, this mobility of population can create sudden pressures and crises at the local level where the final responsibility for providing an education lies.

Urbanization

● As cities grow, students and schools become concentrated and centralized, reducing the opportunities for individual development and increasing the effect of poverty and deprivation.

Fourth Concern: MONEY

Greater need for financial support

● As the educational system becomes larger and more complex, the costs of developing and operating it require a larger percentage of federal, state, and community resources than in the past.

Competition for funds

● The school was once one of the major recipients of community funds. Now many other demands are made by society and government. From national defense to space exploration, the competition for funds is intense.

Accelerated antiquation

● Education as a dynamic function of society creates obsolescence within its system. More money is required to not only maintain the educational system, but for its rejuvenation and revitalization.

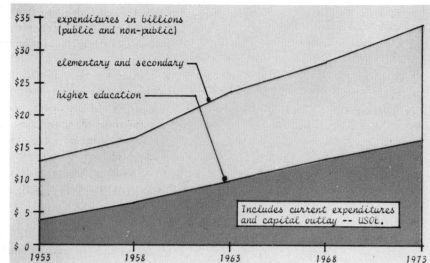

expenditures in billions
(public and non-public)

elementary and secondary

higher education

Includes current expenditures
and capital outlay -- USOE.

Responses to concerns give direction

These, then, are the concerns of contemporary education; it is the response to these concerns that gives direction to the educational system of the country. The detailed translation of these responses into curricula, methods, media and organizational patterns in turn sets the needs for school buildings.

Local direction

In response to these concerns there are several discernible directions in education today. Since education is still a local matter, all these directions are not equally apparent everywhere. To some degree, however, directions in QUALITY, EFFICIENCY, and INDIVIDUALI-ZATION are found in the mainstream of contemporary education. Some may feel that these, if any, are also the objectives of education.

A Direction: QUALITY

Depth and scope

- Education is providing learning opportunities of greater scope and in greater depth than ever before.

Learning principles

- Schools are educating for the understanding of principles *ala* rather than facts in order to develop a thinking population *Bruner* prepared to spend the rest of their lives learning.

Esthetic experience

- There is recognition of the need to develop esthetic experience in order to broaden our cultural base and to enrich individual lives.

Continuing education

- Education is assuming an obligation to treat formal schooling as a beginning rather than a terminus; continuing education is becoming a part of our daily lives. This will aid in solving problems due to technological obsolescence, leisure, and old age.

Increasing effectiveness

- Instruction is now giving attention to techniques and materials for more effective presentation of facts and experiences in order that each segment of learning be valuable and rewarding.

A Direction: EFFICIENCY

More education to more people

- Education is developing more efficient instructional processes to enable bringing more education to more people in wider range and in greater depth.

- There are increased efforts to improve utilization of expensive facilities and human talent.

A Direction: INDIVIDUALIZATION

Four objectives

Four points summarize the direction of education with respect to the individual:

- Encouragement of individual initiative, responsibility and motivation, so that learning becomes person-centered rather than people-centered.

- Development of individual interests and special abilities to allow the individual to establish his appropriate and useful role in society.

- Accommodation of differing individual capacities for learning as well as social and economic backgrounds within the total framework of formal education.

- Development of a sense of personal identification and participation in the learning process, as well as basic learning skills which may be applied in personal learning and self-education.

*Allow students
to grow
educationally*

Others have identified these directions by saying, "The role of the school then becomes, in effect, a learning center, a warehouse of knowledge, a central storage bank for pupils to come and grow as tall educationally as their own potential and their own abilities permit.'[5]

*Mass assembly
education*

"I believe we're all concerned with the present system of education that represents something akin to Detroit's mass assembly line. I don't believe it's anything like that which was conceived by our forefathers, who were trying to plan an educational system to develop people for a country that respected individuality—to train people to grow up as great individuals and to pursue knowledge."16

Now to review these responses, these directions, by reviewing innovations in contemporary education—and the role of learning media.

3 INNOVATIONS IN EDUCATION: ROLE OF MEDIA

The innovation explosion

It has been indicated that the concerns of our time—numbers, knowledge, society, and money—are reflected in the directions of contemporary education. Response to these concerns, resulting in new directions in education, are found in an explosion of new ideas, new approaches, new techniques and new learning materials. These educational innovations, the roles that media play in them, and the implications for facilities, should be analyzed by the policy-maker before making building decisions.

Discuss broad groupings of innovations

Before discussing the roles of learning media as innovative factors themselves, it would be helpful to briefly identify several significant innovations. No attempt will be made to describe the innovation in detail, except in terms of the use of media. While the number and variety of innovations are great, they can be classed in some broad groups,

- GROUPING: differentiating student groups for variety in learning.

- CURRICULA: revising curricula for individual differences.

- TIME: reorganizing the time spent in learning.

- STAFF: restructuring staff for more effective teaching.

- ADMINISTRATION: planning for effective administration.

- RESOURCES: providing students with the required learning resources.

- SYSTEMS: synthesizing the elements of learning.

- MEDIA: increasing the opportunities for learning.

GROUPING: Differentiating Student Groups for Variety in Learning

*Importance of
small groups*

PROJECT AND SEMINAR GROUPS. Bringing students together in small-group situations permits a variety of experiences, many of them made possible by media. They may discuss concepts presented to them in large-group or individual instruction, they may view taped lectures, see re-runs, watch demonstrations, use special media, work with models, miniaturizations, and so on.

*Media used
extensively with
large groups*

LARGE-GROUP INSTRUCTION. Whether the teacher is in the same room with the large-group or he is being presented "on-the-air", media will play a significant part in the success of the presentation. Materials must be clear, pertinent and well displayed; teachers should be able to tape and criticize their lectures and various magnification devices may be necessary. Large group instruction probably provides the greatest potential for the use of many forms of media.

*Media aids multi-
class teaching*

MULTI-CLASS TEACHING: Through the multi-class concept a school can provide many more courses or cover several grades utilizing the same basic resources. In this kind of learning situation, a teacher may have several different groups in the same room at the same time. It is through the use of media that multi-class teaching can be made more effective. Some students may be using programmed instruction, others may be grouped around a TV monitor, while still others review projected materials.

*Media production
serving an entire
park*

EDUCATIONAL PARKS. This approach to putting many levels of education (sometimes pre-school to junior college) on the same site is gathering popularity as a means of solving many educational and social problems. The educational park gives schools the opportunity to invest in extensive media and to share them among the units in the park. For greatest effectiveness, the park will probably contain its own production and origination facilities, and a network for the distribution of resources.

Planning to combat bigness

SCHOOLS-WITHIN-SCHOOLS. Breaking down large educational institutions into smaller and more manageable "houses" or "little schools" is a common solution to the problems of bigness. Decentralization, however, focuses emphasis on networks for distributing instructional materials, and utilization of media in a variety of group sizes and learning situations.

CURRICULA: Revising Curricula for Individual Differences

Allowing for individual differences.

IN GRADED SCHOOLS. Within the framework of the graded school, many attempts have been made to individualize curricula in recognition of student differences in learning rates and capacities. Many of the individual student progress plans are based on taking certain segments of instruction and allowing students to move through them at their own rates. All the attempts set aside a portion of the student's time for independent study. To implement these plans, schools are relying on various forms of media: televised instruction, cartridge films, miniaturized materials, and programmed instruction.

Media aiding nongradedness

IN NONGRADED SCHOOLS. To date, the concept of nongrading or continuous progress through schools has come closest to providing truly individualized instruction. As the traditional structures of schooling (the lecture, the classroom, the period) are changed to accommodate individual progress, the roles of media and planning for media will increase. The problems of instructing and evaluating students on an individual basis, and scheduling resources, are now being solved to a great extent by the use of media, some of which are computer-based. This seems to be one of the most pronounced trends in education today, and every indication is that it will continue to gain momentum and drive.

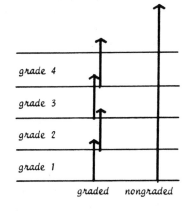

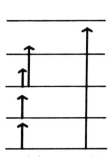

◁ In the nongraded school, fast learners can move at their own pace; do more than a year's work in a school year.

In the nongraded school, slow learners can move at their own pace; do less than a year's work in a school year. ▷

TIME: Reorganizing the Time Spent in Learning

*50-minute period
no longer sacred*

BREAKING DOWN THE TIME PERIOD. As educators attempt to provide a variety of learning experiences and to individualize instruction, the traditional 50-minute time block is being changed. Some schools are extending it, others are making it into a shorter module (from which to build periods of many lengths); others are eliminating it altogether. This trend greatly complicates scheduling; some schools are using computers to straighten out the scheduling of students, teachers, facilities, and media resources. As the time blocks are further dissolved, it will be necessary to provide some learning media on a "random-access" basis.

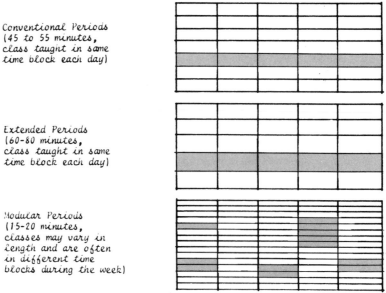

Conventional Periods
(45 to 55 minutes,
class taught in same
time block each day)

Extended Periods
(60-80 minutes,
class taught in same
time block each day)

Modular Periods
(15-20 minutes,
classes may vary in
length and are often
in different time
blocks during the week)

*Schools operating
longer*

EXTENDING SCHOOL DAY, WEEK AND YEAR. The emphases on continuity in learning and better utilization of resources are keeping educational buildings operating longer. Again, this requires easy access to learning materials and media at all times of the day, week and year. Learning doesn't stop at 3:30 P.M.; neither can the access to learning materials.

STAFF: Restructuring Staff for More Effective Instruction

*Teachers and staff
being organized
differently*

In order to provide more effective instruction, new staff organizations, echelons, teams and specialties are appearing. These approaches are reflected in team planning, team teaching and the Trump Plan.

New staff patterns have two important implications for teachers: first, they must rely on more learning media to aid them in bringing variety to instruction and to free them to become directors or counselors of learning, team leaders, etc.; secondly, they must learn to get together and plan for more integrated programs. It is becoming more and more important that teachers receive instructional "support" in the form of local production centers, regional provision of materials and services, opportunities for in-service work, and far greater access to professional resources for their own work. These new staff structures are also producing new kinds of teachers: specialists in multi uses of media, learning programmers, etc.

ADMINISTRATION: Planning for Efficient Administration

*Innovations
complicate
administration*

Nearly all innovations in education have one point in common; they tend to complicate the life of the administrator. A greater variety of student groupings, new staff organizations, schedules that change every week or every day, new facilities types, and new uses of time are forcing him to investigate new administrative techniques. Many institutions have explored computer solutions for scheduling, reporting, testing, and so on, and are, in turn, investigating the use of these computers for actual instructional uses.

RESOURCES: Providing Students with Required Learning Resources

*Resources for
ready use*

The need to provide a "warehouse" of learning resources—books, slides, charts, film clips, tapes, media of all kinds—for the student to use in learning is a common thread winding through nearly all of the innovations in modern education. There are two aspects to the matter of providing resources. First, ways and means of producing more and more resources for teacher and student must be devised. Second, ways to recall those already-produced resources for instant use must be sought.

*Developing learning
materials within
the school...*

While there is already a great variety of instructional materials available on the commercial market, it is also important to provide the teacher and student some local means for producing materials for immediate or special uses. There must be some kind of facility in the school itself, requiring little or no supervision, where staff and students alike can come and produce relatively unsophisticated materials; many schools have done this already.

*...and on a
regional basis*

There is also a trend toward increasing regional development of instructional aids and media. All over the country schools are making efforts to pool resources, hire more professional staff, and produce or originate materials and media for local use. Some of these regional organizations have grown into highly-structured units with a large budget and professional staff; others are just starting. New federal support will certainly lend impetus to the development of regional services.

*Improving
accessibility of
materials*

It is not enough to provide more and better learning resources; they must be made conveniently available to those who are going to use them. Our historic concept of making learning materials available in only one area of the school—the library—and forcing students to come there is changing. No longer are these materials ancilliary to learning; they are learning. As such, the student must be able to get to them quickly and easily.

"(I see the resource center) as an individual study carrel situation backed by a warehouse of knowledge with reference materials, tapes, and so forth, that can be wired into the student's study carrel. Many of these carrels will be in the resource center, but many of them, of course, will be out in various study areas. ....As we continue to grow towards greater independence in learning, we see this resource center move out into what we now call our classroom areas."[5]

SYSTEMS: Snythesizing the Elements of Learning

*Systems analyses
as a major trend*

"Possibly today's major trend...is the application of systems engineering analysis to the educational process. ...Educators are beginning to realize that there is more than one way to reach desired objectives in the primary areas of logistics-the manner of presenting information to the student, and economics-the available resources, with which to accomplish this."[22]

*Learning more
than combining
elements*

The learning situation is far more than the mere collection of elements; it only gains real effectiveness when the elements are put together to encourage desired learning. This process of combining into their most effective patterns is called a "systems" approach. The systems concept asks: what are we trying to do? what is the best way to do it? is this the best way for everyone concerned? is it the best utilization of resources? The same questions are asked whether the preparation of a single unit of material, a sequence of of courses or an entire curriculum, are involved. Of course, the answers become more complicated as we move from simple to more complex situations.

The systems approach is nothing very new; thoughtful educators have been using it in limited situations for years. Only now, with developments in research and evaluation, has anyone been able to apply it on any kind of scale.

MEDIA: Increasing the Opportunities for Learning

Roles of media

The importance of media in designing learning which has greater opportunities for meeting objectives and which represents an effective application of systems analysis is basic. This contention can be supported by noting the many roles that media can and do play in contemporary education.

Do things that couldn't be done before...

- Media can do things—can create learning situations—that cannot otherwise be accomplished (like bringing current events into the classroom).

Present information in new ways...

- Information can be presented in a variety of ways, which best meet particular learning objectives.

...to varying groups

- By varying the medium, information can be presented to groups of many differing sizes—from individuals to national audiences—and it can be presented simultaneously to these differing audiences.

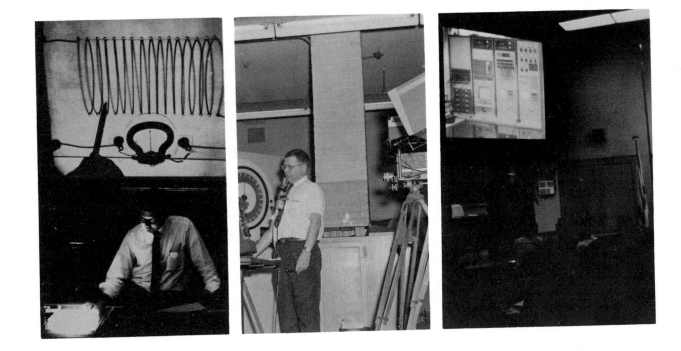

Increase effectiveness

- Media can make learning more effective by increasing the realism, the dynamics, and the emotionalism of information; it can increase the motivation to learn.

Broaden coverage

- Some media, such as television, can make the best teachers and learning situations available to more students.

Extend limitations

- They can extend the limitations of the learning situation by reinforcing and expanding the experience and background of teacher and student. In addition, they can extend limitations imposed by school plant and geographical location.

Permit industrialization

- Media can allow for individualization of curricula by presenting the same information, or variations, to different students at different times.

Releasing teacher time

- They can allow students to work under many situations without teacher guidance or supervision, freeing him for individual assistance.

Accelerate learning

- Education can be made more efficient by using media to direct information to some people in shorter-than-conventional periods of time.

Introduce economics

- Some educational objectives can be realized more economically by using media rather than by conventional means.

Examine goals

- The demands on our educational system require that every possible means of up-grading education be explored. The use of media forces educators to examine their goals and objectives more closely than before.

Educational guidelines

Before leaving this general review of educational innovation to discuss the current status and future of media, it should be recognized that several educational guidelines must be considered when utilizing learning media.

Plan for the use of media

- The educator must fully understand and appreciate the capabilities and limitations of media, and must carefully plan for their effective use.

Design learning

- The kinds and combinations of media and their duration of use should be defined in terms of desired learning objectives and by application of systems analysis techniques.

And most important at this point,

Provide proper facilities

- Appropriate facilities must be provided and must be carefully designed to permit effective uses of media within the broad spectrum of education.

INNOVATIONS IN EDUCATION – A RANDOM LISTING

Grouping Students

Frequent regrouping
Variations in grouping
Independent study and projects
Small-group study and projects
Large groups in single lecture spaces
Large groups in multiple spaces
Large groups via radio and television
Flexible groupings
Multi-age and multi-class groupings
Stay-at-home learning
Pyramidal groupings
Little schools and schools-within-schools
Redeployment plans
Educational parks
Middle schools

Designing Curricula

Homogeneous and heterogeneous tracking
Independent learning
Elective sequences
3- and 4-track plans
Core curricula
Enrichment programs
Nongrading and continuous progress
  methods
Home study and correspondence courses
Job retraining
Special programs for the gifted, disabled,
  handicapped, and culturally-deprived
Continuing or broadening education
Pre-school programs
Learning systems analysis
Cooperative "work-learn" programs
Regional curriculum development projects
Curriculum study groups (PSSC, SMSG, etc.)

Organizing Time

Accommodating variable groupings
Individualized scheduling
New scheduling cycles
Extended and modular class periods
Frequent or continuous rescheduling
Student-planned class periods
Extended school day and week
Evening courses
Summer school remedial and enrichment
  programs
Full school year
Trimester and quartermester plans
Co-operative "work-learn" plans

Utilizing Staff

Team planning and teaching
Discipline-oriented teacher teams
Multi-discipline teacher teams
Teacher cycling
In-service training programs
Echelon organizations
New teacher types and specialists
Teacher aids and assistants
Regional adjunct or supplementary staff

Improving Administration

Computer-based scheduling and registration
Automated data processing for routine work
Tracking and evaluation techniques
Automated test-scoring
Simulation models and techniques
Systems design of school administration
Regional administrative assistance
Space and resource utilization studies
Library mechanization
Computer-based requisitioning and inventory

Expanding Resources and Media

Systems approaches to using media
New types of printed and graphic materials
Programmed textbooks
New "write-on" surfaces
Audio and video recording equipment
Local, regional, international radio
Telephone and Tele-Lecture communication
Language and audio laboratories
Sound slides and filmstrips
Single-concept films
Film catridge projectors
Overhead, opaque and micro-projectors
Systems of audio and projection components
School and regional distribution systems
Miniaturized aids
Student response systems
Commercial educational television
Closed-circuit and 2500 mc television
Airborne distribution systems
Teaching kits
Computer-assisted instruction
Simulation techniques
Computer-based resource listing and handling
Regional resource collections
Regional production of instructional aids
Regional broadcast origination
Information Storage and Retrieval

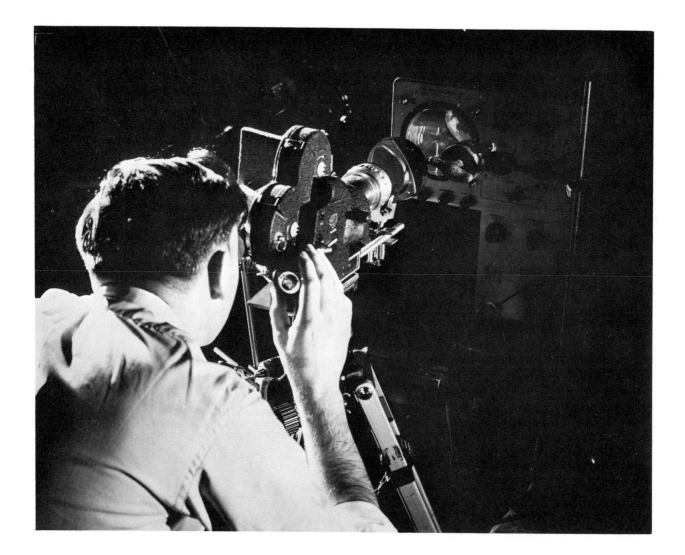

4 LEARNING MEDIA: STATUS AND TRENDS

*Relative
impact of
media*

The development of learning media has certainly had an impact on contemporary education. However, the impact is relative, depending on where you sit. For the parent concerned with reading, writing and arithmetic for his child, there probably is too much television and too many movies, teaching machines and educational hardware. For the media specialist, for the person responsible for the development of media, their adoption and expansion seem painstakingly slow and overwhelmingly limited.

*Statistics
misleading*

Certainly statistics won't tell the whole story — the number of television sets in American schools is a poor measure of the impact and utilization of television, just as the number of film projectors sold or the number of films distributed during a school year is an ineffective measure of the real role these things play in creating better education.

*Status and
trends
important for
planning*

Regardless of the problems involved, a review of current status and trends in the use of learning media is necessary to aid the policy-maker in the realistic development of a school building project. These following points have been gleaned from seminars, talks, papers, discussions, field trips and current literature.

*Uses of media
not yet extensive*

1. In spite of all that is said and written, learning media are not being employed extensively in American Education. For every classroom with an overhead projector, there are hundreds without one. Conventional education of the "2x4x6"* variety still predominates; effective uses of media in new ways is rare. Less than 1% of our total educational budget is spent for learning media and instructional aids.

"..When we...talk to people who are emotionally involved and committed to the values that we see in the field of instructional technology, we might think that a great deal is going on in the country; we're not very realistic about how little is being done. When we talk about the efforts being made here and there, we must realize, I think, that one sparrow does not make a summer."13

Importance of by-products

2. In spite of such small actual usage, learning media have had a surprisingly large impact on education. Investigations of their potential value have called forth curriculum studies, course revisions, redefinition of educational goals, review of the library's role, establishment of basic learning objectives, employing systems analysis techniques in designing learning and a list of other significant and healthy by-products.

More tools for teachers

3. Through learning media the classroom teacher and college professor, and the individual student, now have at their disposal an array of devices to help achieve learning objectives. For the creative and motivated teacher, this is a challenge and an opportunity; the uninspired and uncreative will remain largely unaffected.

Outside support encourages media usage

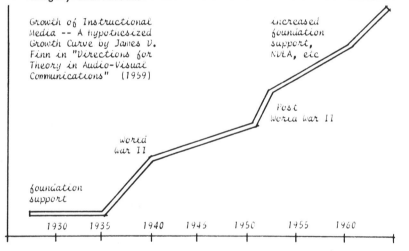

Growth of Instructional Media -- A hypothesized Growth Curve by James D. Finn in "Directions for Theory in Audio-Visual Communications" (1959)

increased foundation support, NDEA, etc

Post World War II

World War II

foundation support

1930 1935 1940 1945 1950 1955 1960

4. Federal, state, and foundation support and industrial promotion have brought the use of learning media to present status. Nothing indicates that such support and promotion will be withdrawn; if anything, they are being expanded. However, without such incentive it seems doubtful that American education would have espoused learning media as extensively as it has.

---

*2 covers of the book, 4 walls of the classroom, 6 periods of the day.

*Media not
taking over*

5. The use of learning media is not "taking over" education; teachers will not be replaced by technology. Media broadens the spectrum of education; they do not, of themselves, provide an education. Even the most media-oriented educators recognize limits and valid restrictions, and are simply trying to establish the most appropriate roles for media within the total educational process.

*Logistic
impediments
to use*

6. The teacher interested in using media today is faced with some real burdens — complicated and costly equipment, poor maintenance, inadequate supply of parts and replacements, immobility of equipment, lack of technical assistance, and improper facilities. Add to this the problems of finding the assistance and the time to learn to use media well; it is surprising that teachers and professors use media at all. These basic logistical problems must be solved school by school, teacher by teacher.

*Segmented approach
to media*

7. Utilization and administration of media are often fragmented; in fact, the development of media has been a history of audio-visual cults. An integrated, multi-media approach has only recently been recognized as significant for success.

At last the film makers, the television specialists, the graphic artists, and the others are being brought together physically, administratively and philisophically. This is the first requisite for a systems approach to learning and for significant multi-media usage.

*Systems concept
with the
proper
administration*

"We're going to have to get away from a fractional approach to media in which the library and its book materials compete with other components for budget, recognition and attention. The systems concept, which cuts across existing boundaries and brings all major operating systems into one functional organization, is what education is going to adopt. I think we're going to find that all boundaries between media units —

library, TV and radio, A-V, graphics, etc. — are going to be cut across, and all media units are going to be brought together. The reason, I think, is obvious. All of these media units exist for a common purpose, — to provide the materials, the services, and the skills so that effective teaching and learning may take place."25

Selection of equipment

8. The amount of hardware available, the types and variations in equipment and the number of functions they can perform, are increasing and will continue to increase at a rapid rate. Unfortunately there is a tendency in selecting instructional equipment to overlook the need for matching the electrical characteristics and interconnection provisions of "hardware" items. Thus, in many instances a school may find itself in possession of an oversupply of mutually incompatible items and will lack the facilities needed to implement its overall instructional program.

Staff members responsible for the selection of instructional media hardware must keep themselves fully informed concerning the availability of equipment and components of interest to their institution. They should be fully qualified to match product functions and performance capabilities of equipment with requirements for achieving learning. In turn, industry will become more responsive to the needs of education as education becomes a major market for hardware.

Single, versatile distribution system

9. The greatest need is the development of a single, economical system for the distribution of good quality audio and color video. When such a system is available for inter-connecting facilities in buildings, between buildings, and between institutions, then the ready availability of resources will become reality. The input for such a system must be highly flexible to include three dimensional, moving and still materials; the output or reception must be equally appropriate for individuals, small groups, and large groups.

Significance of recording devices

10. There is now a variety of audio-video recording devices. When these become completely dependable, inexpensive, and available for color, then some significant changes in technique and methods can be realized. No longer will live demonstrations in the sciences be necessary; finally the benefits of the field trip can be realized without the problems of moving large numbers of students away from the school; and broadcast television will become useful at the school level through recording and local use at appropriate times. Each independent school and teacher will be able to structure the use of mass media to fit a particular system of education.

*Equipment
of individual use*

11. Equipment will be perfected and economically feasible for making media available for learning on an individual student basis. Films, tape, and slide materials will be as easily used and as inexpensive as printed books. This will bring together the two most significant trends in education — individualized instruction and use of learning media.

*People to do
things for
themselves*

"If we are talking individualization seriously, we will, of course, put all the materials under the total control of the individual. All these new systems anticipate making it completely possible for people to do things by themselves. Otherwise, individualization doesn't mean anything when you translate it into principles for media development."3

*Teachers better
prepared*

12. The future should see the classroom teacher better prepared for and more sympathetic toward the use of media in day by day instruction. Schools of education will revamp or broaden their curricula, more in-service programs will be provided, and the teacher will find wide professional acceptance of media.

*Development
of media
specialists*

13. Because of the intellectual challenge and potential creativity necessary to meet the challenges of media in education, a specialty group of educators will develop which is highly skilled and highly motivated in their uses. These persons will be more than technicians; they will be media-pedagogists who will plan and design learning situations that will bring the greatest value from media. These specialists will be supported, as will all teachers, by technicians knowledgeable in hardware, its operation, maintenance, and repair.

*The supporting
team*

Rounding out the supporting team will be the production specialists well versed in effective television production, film making, graphic production, programming, audio recording and radio.

*Information
retrieval
systems*

14. In response to amassing information and the uses of media will come economical systems for storing and calling up information. However, these systems will be developed and will become practical only for information for which there is great demand. It is inconceivable that there will ever be a time when all information, regardless of remoteness and limited application, will be readily accessible through high speed retrieval systems. Dial-up systems for desired information are coming, but the information dialed will be of the "ready reference" type.

*Practical
limitations to
retrieval
systems*

"We've been reading a lot of things lately by people who propose complex systems of dialing so that the student will be able to sit in his carrel and have access to any recorded information that he needs, simply by dialing it. If you analyze it, though, this becomes a very complicated production and design problem. Let's say that there are maybe 2,000 items — tapes, films, etc. — to which a child in a carrel should have access. The ideal thing, and I think what many of us assume when we think of an ultimate dial system, is to have an infinite number of information sources all in operating mode all at the same time. This is an impossibility. There will have to be compromises all along the line to make this kind of system practical."[7]

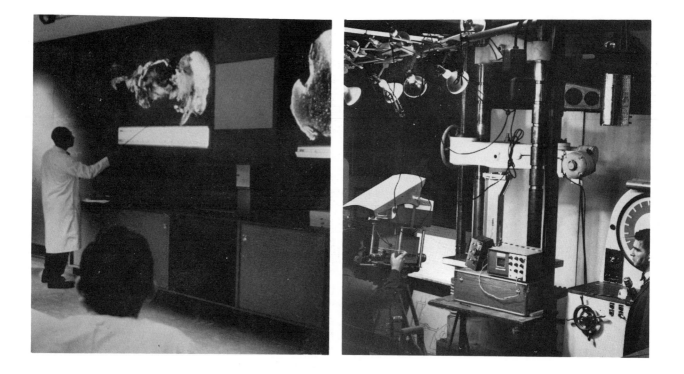

*Media used
in many ways*

15. Information in many forms will be available for use in many different kinds of learning situations. The current emphasis on the learning resources center has created a new concept of use. In addition, media will be used in case studies, in seminars, in laboratories, in shops, in recreational areas, and in the many specialized facilities that make up the school and college. They will be available for learning of many types and variations, and will not be restricted only to mass instruction or independent study.

*Role of research
and evaluation*

16. If any one development is necessary in media, it is the expanded use of a systems approach for the design and planning of learning to enable using media in the most creative and beneficial way. This implies extensive educational research and evaluation (possibly some of our great data processing potential can be turned to analyzing the results of experimentation), and equipment developed in response to need based on extensive research in the uses of media. Some such research must occur in the teachers colleges in order for them to establish a forefront role in education.

*Costs of
media*

17. And what about the costs of educational research and development? Some find them prohibitive and impeding. Others feel more optimistic.

   "We talk about the cost. We have perhaps two million students taking ninth grade algebra, in our country. If we could devote $1,000,000 to developing an instructional system for the best possible method we can design for teaching algebra, we could amortize this cost of $1,000,000, just to take a rough figure, at 50¢ per student in only one year. Think what we could do with 2 or 3 or 4 years. So, I think our cost barriers are rather questionable." 13

In summary, the trends indicate an expanded role for media in many more kinds of learning situations. More equipment, doing more things more economically is part of the future, as are teachers and specialists with unique roles in the development and use of media. There is also need for conscious effort in designing learning to make the most effective use of media and to develop media to meet well-established performance criteria and roles. All of these have significant implications for school building design.

5 LEARNING MEDIA: IMPLICATIONS FOR PLANNING

Implications for staff, leadership, budget and facilities

For the policy-maker who must assume decisions for both educational and building programs, the uses of media in contemporary education have a wide range of implications that he must consider at the outset of planning. These implications will affect such areas as staffing, leadership, budget, and facilities. Considering the nature of this report, more attention will be given to the last area.

Staff Implications

Staff attitudes and readiness for uses of media

It has already been suggested that the teaching and supporting staffs play a key role in the use of media. With a commitment to the use of learning media, it is up to the administrator to lead and direct his staff into the development of attitudes, skills and programs which will make the use of media effective and efficient. This may involve developing in-service programs and demonstration projects, remodeling existing classrooms, and providing support staff, technical assistance and production facilities. The administrator and staff must develop an attitude of co-operation in planning for the uses of media.

Leadership Implications

Initial leadership and follow-through

The use of media in education can only be accomplished through strong and thorough educational leadership. The administrator or policy-maker must not only be willing to "get the ball rolling" but to keep it moving. More than one institution has suffered the consequences of the over-zealous administrator who got everyone motivated to undertake a new approach to education, only to see it falter from lack of continued attention.

*Leadership at
the local level*

It is another criticism of many systems and institutions that administrative leadership becomes ineffective when translated at the local level. An all-too-common example of this can be found in many large school systems; there will be leadership at the superintendent's level, but the local "A-V" co-ordinator is a full-time teacher with a part-time "A-V" load. As a result, this key man cannot exert the necessary local leadership.

If an institution adopts a serious approach to using media extensively in teaching and learning, then the staff charged with the diagnosis and treatment of learning problems must be particularly competent. And, just as importantly, they must be given the time, the financial resources, and the facilities to accomplish this leadership role.

Budget Implications

*Media reflected
in operating
budgets and...*

As media play an increased role in education, there will be budget implications that the administrator cannot avoid. The cost of materials and equipment will assume a larger share of the operating budget, and budgets are going to have to become "flexible" enough to allow for research, evaluation, and change. Likewise, hardware and facilities and will need continual updating in the face of new developments.

*...building
budgets*

Not only does the utilization of media imply an initial investment in hardware, and budgetary provision for change, but it further adds to the growing percent of the building dollar that goes for equipment. "I think that undoubtedly the ratio between the cost of the structure and cost of its equipment will increase on the side of the equipment. It is increasing. For a long time, you know, we thought we could equip a building for 10% of the cost of the structure, but I think that day has passed. We've got to think about financing all of this new equipment that is needed for the utilization of new media."[6]

Facilities Implications

*Foolish to
ignore media*

It would be foolish to ignore learning media when planning contemporary facilities. Even if no immediate uses are planned, or if only minor uses are to be incorporated immediately, media will eventually be used during the life span of the building. Such future uses must be anticipated and planned; to ignore them will create handicaps and may actually prohibit the future effective use of media.

*Define present
and future
uses*

When a building program is first being considered the policymaker must define present and potential uses for media in terms of the educational program, the character of the institution, the talents and development of the staff, the type of financial support, the existing institutions throughout the region, and the interests and motivation of taxpayers, alumni, and the other influential groups.   These same factors will be analyzed during the development of the building program (see Part 6 — Programming) but they must be considered initially in terms of learning media utilization.

*Provide facilities
based on analysis
of use*

Once the basic analysis of the role of media has been established, it is then necessary initially to provide facilities which 1.) will support media use, 2.) will provide an appropriate environment for education, and 3.) will later adapt and change as programs and methods change.

*Media usage
requires
special design
considerations
and...*

The planning of school buildings in which media are to be used requires great care in the detailed design and equiping of facilities. Every aspect of the total environment of a space is more critical when it is planned for effective use of media. Lighting, acoustics, seating, shape, color, display surfaces and equipment controls all demand special attention when they make up a learning environment with media.   In fact, it is the knowledge that spaces with media require more critical design and planning than otherwise, that has motivated the preparation of these reports.

*...other types
.of facilities...*

Also it is necessary for the policy-maker to be aware that the uses of media imply additional kinds of facilities not always found in more conventional school buildings:

*...such as a
variety of
spaces
for learning...*

● A variety of spaces in which students, teachers and media can come together in varying configurations. The reason for needing a variety of learning spaces is obvious: extensive use of media impose certain limitations on facilities design, layout, and furnishings. Rather than attempting to accommodate the unique needs of large-group, middle-group, and small-group learning in a single kind of facility, it is probably advisable to recognize the uniqueness of these situations by providing a variety of facility types. "Multi-use spaces too often become multi-useless spaces." Moving students among facilities, each specifically designed to accommodate a particular learning situation, is one answer to the larger concern with "flexibility."

*...planning
spaces...*

● A variety of planning spaces for teachers and staff. Faculties will also use these planning spaces for media preview and evaluation, as well as for coordinating and preparing instruction.

*...and supporting
facilities*

● A variety of supporting facilities, local and regional, for the production and origination of media of all kinds. "I'm not sure that we've emphasized quite enough what the implications may be for what I would refer to as 'supporting' kinds of facilities, but our structures are going to take on quite a different character. We're going to have more space for the production, for the maintenance, for the distribution of these new materials."26

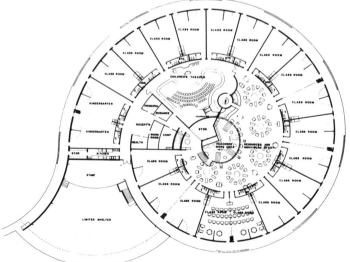

Details in Report B

These various types of space and considerations in their design are covered in detail in Report B — "A Guide for the Design Professions"; it is necessary here for the policy-maker to understand that not only is the design of space more critical, but different types of of space are involved when media are to be used effectively and efficiently.

Educational objectives the basis for planning

Finally, it is possible when planning schools with media, to become too concerned with the details of equipment, budget, administration, and not enough with educational programs. Any planning begins with a definition of educational purpose and intent; educational facilities and equipment are simply part of the means of implementation. Educational goals dictate school planning and design; not equipment or other details. "I think frequently we design facilities to accommodate the hardware. In visiting colleges and universities in various parts of the country, I see an unfortunate rush to get on the bandwagon and build facilities and buy TV projectors and install student response systems because it's the thing to do, even though they don't utilize them effectively or at all. We are building the spaces to accommodate the hardware rather than the students." 25

Programming translates objectives into building needs

With educational objectives defined, and methods and media established, it is the process of architectural programming that establishes the contents and character of the school building.

6 PROGRAMMING: DEFINING BUILDING NEEDS

*Programming
often overlooked
or incomplete*

There is one step in the design and building process for which the administrator and policy-maker must assume prime responsibility: the development of the building program. The development of the program is a vital task, too often incompletely considered or entirely overlooked. A truly successful educational plant can result only from detailed and complete programming.

*Program
describes the
building
in words*

Simply put, the building program is a statement from the administrator translating the school's philosophy and goals into building requirements. It defines with words and diagrams the people and functions to be accommodated, the kinds of facilities needed, and their relationships to each other. The program, as a printed document, appears deceptively simple, but programming is a complex process. It involves many groups often with conflicting or parochial interests — teachers, staff, administrators, taxpayers, other "influential" groups and committees. It involves complex, often conflicting statements of goals, philosophy and policy. It involves complicated financial, political and administrative factors. It involves hard work and diplomacy. For these reasons programming is often forfeited in favor of arbitrary, but painless, decisions.

*The building
program gives
general
background...*

The building program should give the architect all basic necessary information about the building he is to design. It should first include,

- A clear statement of the institution's educational philosophy, and the significance of the proposed building in the light of these goals and objectives.

- A more definitive statement of the purpose of the building, and its role in the district, the campus or the community.

- A brief description of the functions that will be going on in the building, particularly if they deviate from more historic functions.

...and specific details

In short, this background part of the building program should give the architect what might be called a "feel" for the building and its role in the educational process. From this base, it can become more specific:

- A schedule of every desired space in the building defining the types of users, number of users, functions to be housed, required square footages, necessary furniture, required equipment, and other supporting functions. All special requirements of which the architect should be aware should be included.

- A description of how each of the spaces will relate to each other and to the building as a whole.

- Analysis of how the building functions as a whole. This includes information about access, circulation, and overall servicing needs.

Educational specification and the building program

Sometimes the building program is not the single document or closely related documents implied here, but is composed of two separate entities — the educational specifications and the architectural program. The educational specs will contain the educational philosophy, purposes, and functions, while the architectural program will be the definitive statement of space types and design features.

Program is a method of communication

In any case, the building program gives a complete, concise, and accurate description of the building and all of its parts. It is the basic document upon which the architect begins his work. The architect looks at it this way; "We look to the educator to say how to teach, and what equipment to teach with, and then it's our responsibility to provide the housing — the outside limitations of walls, ceilings and roofs to control the elements — and to create an environment which is conducive to the learning process and will not stand in the way of it."29

Decisions behind the program

It is not difficult to realize why the task of developing a building program is so difficult that it is often by-passed or left to arbitrary or non-committal decisions. Its development requires many decisions, decisions which go to the very heart of the educational institution:

Types of questions

- What are the educational objectives of the program to be housed in this building, and how do these relate to the rest of the institution or school system?

- What curriculum or curriculum elements must be accommodated in the building?

- What instructional methods and techniques will be employed?

- What types of students will be housed? How many? What age levels?

- What types of staff will use the building? How will this staff be structured?

- What special services and resources will be necessary to support the educational program?

- How will learning be scheduled? How will the building be utilized? How long will it be open?

- What administrative organizations will be functioning within or over this building?

- What basic types of facilities will be necessary to carry out the educational programs?

- How will each of these items change in time, and what should be done about this in terms of facilities?

No simple answers

These are not simple "yes" and "no" decisions that can be easily made. Many hours of debate, many shades of opinion, and some calculated guesswork will enter into all these decisions, decisions that will become the basis for specific requirements spelled out in the program.

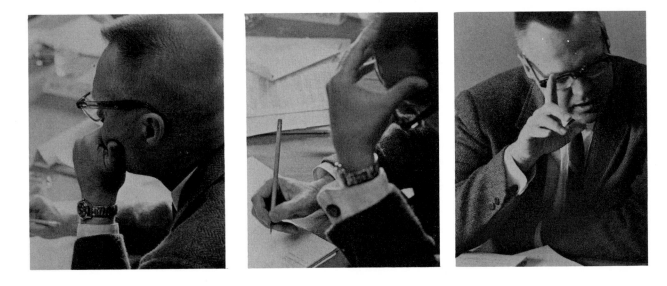

Who makes the decisions and supervises the process?

The manner in which the program is actually developed varies from school to school. Some institutions rely on an outside consultant who develops the building program, working in close contact with the faculty, staff and administration. Some designate an administrative officer as responsible (an assistant superintendent or in larger institutions, a co-ordinator of planning). Other schools and institutions undertake the process through committees of faculty and staff. More and more schools are relying on their architect to undertake the programming as an extension of his architectural services. Perhaps a new type of specialist is needed; "We should try to prepare a new professional person, new in the sense that he will incorporate the knowledge of the educator with the insights of the architect. Such a man might very well be on the staff of every architectural firm which aspires to build educational buildings."26

While there is no "best" way to approach the problem, there are certain general principles that might be kept in mind:

Time for programming

- The programming process needs, above all, time — time to see that it is done completely and thoroughly, and represents the best work of all involved.

  "We need a willingness on the part of the faculty to become involved in the planning of facilities. Unless they have something to do with the planning from the very beginning, they will have little interest in the later stages of the facility development. All too often we expect our faculty to plan on their own time and do not allow them any extra time for this important process. These activities demand budgeted planning funds and a variety of resources."24

Involve the architect

- The architect should be involved in the programming process. Not only can he lend professional assistance and aid in the process, but by becoming involved in the early stages he will have a better understanding of the needs and problems behind the program.

  "We find, that there isn't enough time allowed for the planning process. People go without a school for years and years; then all of a sudden they want it built yesterday and the architect gets caught. If we're going to build a school in 1968, we try to get the people to start on it right now."15

Overall responsibility

- The administrator or policy-maker should assume, or appoint some one person to assume, overall direction of the process.

Involve the faculty

- Even though all faculty and staff will not have useful and contributive opinions, they should nevertheless be asked to state their views. This fosters a spirit of participation in the process, and will forestall many problems later; people find it hard to disavow decisions in which they had some say.

*Take advantage
of data processing*

- Data processing and analysis should be employed whenever practical in programming. "Computer models" can simulate schedules, traffic flows, functions, operations and interactions, and can develop high levels of staff and facilities utilization. These techniques can be profitably employed to create a technically more competent document.

*Programmer as
diplomat and
referee*

Whoever is in control of the programming process will most likely find himself a mediator or arbiter among the various positions and groups. It is important that this person be extremely capable, for all too many building programs end up manifesting a very strong influence by one person or one small group to the exclusion of others involved. This is a particular problem in colleges and universities where a strong department chairman, a well-known teacher or researcher, or a person who can bring significant financial resources to the institution will often dictate the building form and contents to satisfy personal wishes or biases. When these people leave, which often occurs amazingly soon after the building is completed, the structure (or at least elements of it) are found to be unsuited to the staff and programs remaining behind.

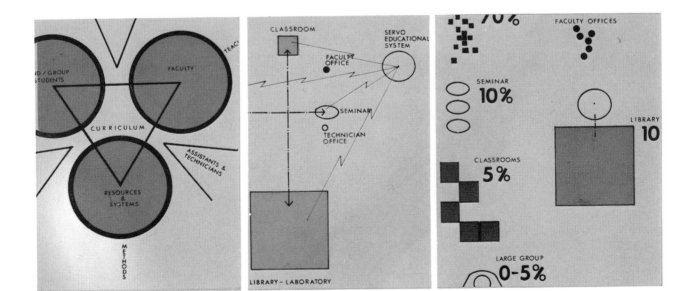

*Other uses for
the program*

The chief purpose of the building program is to serve as a guide and reference document for the architect during the design process. It has a number of other uses, too:

*Stating
objectives*

- By "forcing" staff and administrators to sit down and clearly define needs, objectives are clarified in everyone's mind.

*Paper
changes*

- The program lets everyone know what is to be built, and changes can be made ahead of time, on paper, instead of later during construction or in renovation.

Equipment list

● The program can be used for selecting and purchasing furniture and equipment early in the process.

Estimating

● By defining total areas and equipment needs, the program can give a base for estimates and budgeting.

Policy tool

● The program can be an effective instrument for diplomacy, publicity, development, and the co-ordination of a united effort.

Program like the lesson plan

The building program is to the architect as the lesson plan is to the classroom teacher; without it, the result can be ineffective and wasteful. All that goes into any building is the best informed knowledge brought to bear by the group concerned with it. Programming is the process for insuring this transfer.

APPENDIX A

Three Meetings in May: A Resume

APPENDIX B

Educational Innovation: An Overview

THREE MEETINGS IN MAY: A RESUME

As a means of obtaining a cross-section of authoritative opinion regarding significant current trends in education and their impact on facilities, three invitational seminars were held in Chicago in May 1964. To each of these meetings was invited a small group of knowledgeable men of recognized stature; each group represented a variety of backgrounds and viewpoints—teaching, administration, educational research, architecture, educational resources and facilities research. All of these meetings had the common objective of assessing the appropriate applications and requirements of media in education.

Each of the three meetings dealt nominally with a different level of education: elementary, secondary, higher. This division, while arbitrary, allowed the group to determine the extent of mutual concerns, and to remain small, informal, and productive. Each seminar participant was asked to briefly respond to these questions,

1. What do you see as the significant trends in education in terms of instructional techniques and methods?

2. What roles do you see instructional aids and media playing in each of these trends?

3. What do you see as the resulting implications for educational facilities?

It was not surprising to find that similar philosophies and concerns were expressed, and similar trends indicated at all three seminars. In view of the fact that there had been no preliminary exchange of thoughts, and, in fact, no formal papers prepared, the opinions expressed were mutually supplementary and reinforcing to a surprising degree. Dozens of topics pertinent

to the questions were discussed; it would be impossible to indicate in a summary the wide scope of interests expressed. The following resume, however, will serve to highlight some of the matters of chief concern and to give a brief distillation of views expressed in regard to each.

1. ON NEW THINKING ABOUT EDUCATION...

- Education is becoming a national concern. Sputnik, the new technologies and some key publications have fostered an aura of nation-wide concern for quality and broadened scope.

- More people and rapidly expanding knowledge have caused a feeling of emergency in education.

- The new technologies have shown us what we can do; now the problem becomes applying them effectively in our schools.

- The forces of automation, obsolescence and the explosion of new information is forcing us to accept education as a life-long task. Naturally, then, we want to improve it.

2. ON EDUCATIONAL ROLES...NEW AND OLD...

- Education and our schools are becoming more "world-oriented." The student must be better prepared — intellectually, socially, emotionally — for the roles he will assume in community and nation.

● Learning is becoming a part of the "fabric" of life. Schooling is no longer limited to basic training and skills; it has been extending to retraining, specialized, and continuing education.

● Our schools are extending their horizons to cover all groups — not only the average individual, but also the gifted, the unstable, the deprived.

● The school is still considered the fortress and the regenerator of democracy. Here students learn habits and work-patterns that will guide them through their everyday lives. We must ever temper our enthusiasm for change with this reminder.

3. ON INNOVATION . . . . .

● A proliferation of innovations is the natural result of our varying educational concerns — we must find new ways of doing things.

● Innovation, however, must overcome many problems of its own. Resistance to change, lack of resources, and passive or even obstructive attitudes of teachers, administrators and even the general public are often encountered.

● The process by which an innovation is introduced may be as important as the innovation itself. Many persons may have to be "oriented" toward an innovation before it will be accepted.

● Facilities can promote and encourage innovation, but they should not be relied upon to do the total job.

4. ON THE ROLE OF MEDIA IN INNOVATION . . . .

● Media can play important roles in the innovation process. Certain forms may be just the ticket to make certain ideas click. For instance, neither effective large-group instruction nor effective individual instruction is wholly possible without supporting media.

● The roles for media in an innovation should be considered beforehand. If not properly prepared, the innovation may fail without having had a real chance.

● The use of media can free teachers from constant contact with students. This then allows teachers more time for planning and thinking — often about new innovation.

5. ON THE NEED TO UTILIZE RESOURCES...

- An overwhelming drive today is that of economizing on resources used in learning — teachers, time, materials, facilities. This does not necessarily mean using the cheapest or least expensive approaches however — costly persons and things can be deployed in economical, but effective, patterns.

- The use of media can often increase utilization. Its ability to accommodate different groups in different learning situations — often without the presence of the teacher — is important in this respect.

- Large-group instruction has been effectively used toward these ends. Particularly in colleges and some secondary schools, the large-group has allowed presentation of material to many students at the same time — utilizing the valuable teacher resource and the valuable time resource more efficiently. The large-group lecture also allows, indeed demands, sophisticated presentation techniques.

- Proponents of individualization consider the large-group approach out-of-place in their programs. Others claim that it can only provide one-way communication, but this can be answered with various response and feedback mechanisms.

6. ON RECOGNIZING DIFFERENCES AMONG INDIVIDUALS ....

- There has been a growing recognition of the essential differences among individuals. Schools should exploit these differences rather than submerge them as we have done in the past.

- Students should have the opportunity to learn according to rate and capacity. Individual initiative should be fostered, and students given the latitude to think independently and "learn by doing."

- Responsibility for learning can be transferred from the teacher to the students — just where it belongs. Pupils, in turn, must become aware of these responsibilities.

- Independence should be offered to all students, not just the best or the most highly gifted, although not all students can benefit extensively from independence.

- Individualization places great importance on the social structure of the school. The concept of independence goes hand-in-hand with that of interdependence.

- A whole series of problems associated with individualization must be solved, however. Evaluation, tracking, administration and more complicated educational planning will all be encountered.

7. ON NEW ROLES FOR TEACHERS ....

- Contrary to many popular beliefs, new ideas are not displacing teachers. Many roles are changing however. The teacher is no longer merely a dispenser of knowledge, but an organizer of inquiry as well as acquiry — an inspirer and a co-learner.

- The key-words are co-operation and planning. As teachers break out of the self-contained classroom they must work, confer and plan together. They need spaces in which to do this.

- More special abilities will be required of teachers in the future. They will have to have a firm grasp on educational psychology to fit their roles as "directors" of learning.

- Schools are moving from the custodial situation to one in which students can come and go. The teacher must relinquish the central role in this process and become a teammate or — as one seminar participant put it — a physician who is not constantly present, but always available.

- The teacher plays a key role in the use of media; this role must not be underestimated in introducing innovations which rely on media for their success.

- The new media are forcing educators to sit down and formalize learning objectives; the teacher must be willing to accept this constant "picking apart" of many time-honored concepts.

- Teachers colleges, in the main, lag far behind many developments in the field. This lag unfortunately includes training in effective uses of media.

8. ON NEW ORGANIZATIONAL PATTERNS....

- The need to break out of the 2 x 4 x 6 lockstep (education within the confines of the 2 covers of the textbook, 4 walls of the room, and 6 periods of the day) requires changes in school structure and organization.

- School programs must become flexible enough to accommodate many group sizes and types, many different learning situations.

- Administrators will need help, possibly from the computer, in working out many of these organizational problems.

9. ON COMMUNICATIONS ....

- Communication is the key to learning, and ways and means of accomplishing it are changing in the 1960s.

- We are no longer tied to the "muscles of the teacher's voice box." Rather we can use learning media to bring the student into contact with a wide variety of learning experiences even without the physical presence of the teacher.

- Many of the new forms of communication are one-way, and this is not necessarily bad. Watching a single-concept film or calling up a piece of information can be accomplished effectively in this medium.

10. ON LEARNING "SYSTEMS"...

- As interest in the learning process grows, and as many different ways of accomplishing it are devised, there will be a greater need for overall planning.

- This planning will be embodied in what we are calling a "systems concept" — each piece of information to be conveyed will be looked at in terms of: how can it be best done? by whom? in what size group? using what media? in what facility? and so on.

- An important facet of the systems concept is evaluation. In too many cases we use learning media without ever analyzing them in the light of educational goals.

11. ON THE ROLE OF MEDIA ...

- In general, the role of media in education is expanding. It is being considered a logical route for conveying ideas — both in the large-group situation and in individual access to information.

- As the educational market gains strength and depth, cost factors are decreasing. More media "tailored" to educational needs are coming onto the market, too.

- An increasing share of the building budget will be devoted to media and equipment as time goes on.

- Media will not replace teachers. Rather it will expand learning horizons, aid him in bringing a wide variety of learning experiences, and free him to become more of a learning "counselor."

- Even though the role of media in our schools is on the upswing, attempts to recognize its importance in our teachers colleges are less pronounced. This is a situation in need of correction.

12. ON TELEVISION . . . .

- Of the various instructional media in use today, television remains the most controversial. A variety of opinions — ranging from thorough acceptance to outright disclaim — were exhibited at the meetings.

- Some consider it the "massiest" of the mass mediums, a constant threat to individualization, and a convenient facade behind which we can hide our real concerns.

- Others feel that television — especially when combined with many other functions for which it is suited such as information display, data remoting, etc. — is a particularly viable medium.

- The overall feeling was that we should continue to evaluate television — and indeed any of the other newer media — not on the basis of past performance, but on the basis of what it can do in future performance.

13. ON CENTRALIZING RESOURCES . . . .

- The role of the school library is changing. No longer can we consider it a large repository of books, impenetrable to everyone not armed with a great deal of fortitude and implicit faith in the Dewey Decimal System. The resource center — as we are now calling it — must be a vital thing, accessible to all and easily used.

- The resource center is envisioned as serving two functions: first its historic role as the source of information for research and enrichment, and secondly, as an actual source of instruction.

- This is easier said than done. First we must revise our concept of what a learning resource is. To books and pamphlets we must add a long list of tapes, records, films, programmed texts and other media.

- We must find new ways of classifying these so they can be easily found.

- We must either make them accessible by bringing the student and teacher into the resource center, or by providing elaborate distribution channels throughout the school.

14. ON ACCESSIBILITY AND DISTRIBUTION. . .

- Someone at the meetings suggested that the library "be out on the lawn where people can get to it." This does not necessarily mean that every student and teacher has to be brought into the collection of resources, however. A great deal of thought is being given to methods of distributing material.

- Perhaps educational communications in the school should be treated as a nervous system — a central repository of materials with an extensive "channel" winding through the school. This channel can be tapped anywhere by anyone.

- In any case, there is a need to find ways of bringing information to students and teachers — and to do it without delay and without expensive handling of hardware.

15. ON PRODUCTION AND ORIGINATION . . . .

- As the role of materials and equipment becomes increasingly important in our schools, it is important that both teachers and students be given facilities for production and origination.

- Some provision for local in-school production units should be made — here students and teachers can turn out simple teaching aids at a moment's notice.

● Many schools (and co-operatives of schools) are backing up local production units with regional centers. These regional operations can produce materials for local needs but on a more professional basis.

16. ON PLANNING AND DESIGN . . . .

● Most at the seminars felt that the greatest need in education today is for planning — planning on all levels. As far as facilities go, their planning should be thorough and an extension of the schools educational philosophy.

● In one of the meetings it was suggested that a school be built three times: once by the educator in his program, once by the architect in his planning, and finally by the builder in the appropriate materials. Too often we forget about the first step

● Necessities of passing bond issues and gaining financing have too long perpetrated dull, uninspiring and institutional educational buildings. We must begin to realize that there is "something special" about learning—and it should be reflected in facilities too.

● Schools are becoming more and more a part of their community. As the school day, week and year become longer, and as the school assumes new roles in retraining, broadening and continuing education, school and community begin to form a real partnership.

17. ON PROVIDING A LEARNING ENVIRONMENT . . . .

● Facilities can — and should — do more than house students. The school should provide a real "climate for learning," an environment responsive to student needs and the many different tasks he performs.

● Architects and educators alike have given too little thought to what gives a building "child appeal." Why not different forms of space, different materials, different finishes that will create different sensations of experience?

● It was a prevailing opinion that each student should have a place in the school to call his own, a place to study, to keep his possessions, to receive resources, etc.

● There is need for much more research into the learning environment.

18. ON FACILITIES FOR PLANNING . . . .

● In our drive to provide facilities for learning, we often overlook facilities for planning. Teachers must have spaces where they can confer, discuss and plan— both privately and in groups.

● Teachers and staff should be given the same access to learning resources as is given to students.

19. ON FACILITIES FOR MEDIA . . . .

● The use of media has many implications for facilities — educators and architects would be wise to recognize these at the outset. Small planning changes at the beginning of a project are much more desirable — and much less costly — than major changes after the building is built.

● With respect to using media, there is often a great tendency toward the versatile space — the space that can do "many things." Unfortunately, multi-use spaces all too often become "multi-useless." Thought should be given to designing spaces that perform less functions better.

● More thought should be given to spaces for the production of aids and media within the school.

20. ON PLANNING FOR CHANGE . . . .

- Even though everyone at the meetings recognized that the only real constant in education today is change, there are widely varying opinions on how this should be reflected in facilities.

- There is the "flexibility" camp which suggests that all partitions should go and space in the building be "infinitely changeable."

- Others feel that "flexibility" is an overworked term, a cliche which is too often used to cloud the issues or to hedge against the future.

- Perhaps a compromise — and maybe a new term, "Adaptability" — is the way to describe this essential requirement. We know things will change, and we should accommodate it as easily as possible. We should provide a variety of spaces, some expandable, with a variety of environments. We should construct our schools so these can be changed in time — perhaps from year to year — to allow for changing curricula. We should construct some of them to change from hour-to-hour, some from day-to-day.

ELEMENTARY EDUCATION, Monday, 18 May 1964

PARTICIPANTS

1. Dr. E. W. Rushton
   Superintendent of Schools
   Roanoke City Public Schools
   217 Church Street West
   Roanoke, Virginia

2. John Shaver
   Shaver and Company, Architects
   205 South Santa Fe
   Salina, Kansas

3. Dr. Arthur W. Foshay
   Horace Mann Institute
   Teachers College
   Columbia University
   New York, New York

4. Dr. Frank W. Cyr
   Professor of Education
   Teachers College
   Columbia University
   New York, New York

5. Dr. Nolan Estes
   Superintendent
   Riverview Gardens School District
   St. Louis, Missouri

6. Dr. John W. Gilliland
   Director, School Planning Laboratory
   University of Tennessee
   Knoxville, Tennessee

7. Dr. Rudy Bretz
   Vice President
   Television Systems Planning
   National Education Sciences Corp.
   1360 Los Angeles Street
   Anaheim, California

PROJECT ADVISORY COMMITTEE

8. Dr. William M. Brish
   Superintendent
   Board of Education, Washington County
   Hagerstown, Maryland

SECONDARY EDUCATION, Wednesday, 20, May 1964

PARTICIPANTS

9. Dr. Melvin N. Barnes
    Superintendent of Schools
    Portland Public Schools
    631 Northeast Clackmas Street
    Portland, Oregon

10. Dr. B. Frank Brown
    Principal
    Melbourne High School
    Melbourne, Florida

11. Dr. Philip Lewis
    Director of Educational Research
    Chicago Public Schools
    228 North LaSalle Street
    Chicago, Illinois

12. Dr. John Cogswell
    Systems Development Corporation
    2500 Colorado Avenue
    Santa Monica, California

13. Colonel Gabriel S. Ofeish, USAF
    3 South East Road
    Randolph Air Force Base, Texas

14. John McLeod, F.A.I.A.
    McLeod & Ferrara
    1223 Connecticut Avenue, N.W.
    Washington, D. C.

15. Dr. James D. MacConnell
    Professor of Education
    Director, School Planning Laboratory
    School of Education
    Stanford University
    Stanford, California

16. Dr. Edwin A. Read
    Director, Laboratory School
    Brigham Young University
    Provo, Utah

17. Stephen Berner
    Director, Developmental Services
    Encyclopaedia Britannica Press
    Encyclopaedia Britannica
    425 North Michigan Avenue
    Chicago, Illinois

PROJECT ADVISORY COMMITTEE

18. Dr. John Cameron
    Director
    Administrative Instruction
        Support Branch
    U. S. Office of Education
    Washington, D. C.

19. Marvin R. A. Johnson
    Design Consultant
    Division of School Planning
    State of North Carolina
    Raleigh, North Carolina

PROJECT STAFF, attending all three meetings

Wayne F. Koppes, A.I.A.
Adjunct Professor of Building
    Research
Center for Architectural Research

Morton C. Gassman
Associate Professor of Architecture
Center for Architectural Research

Alan C. Green
Associate Professor of Architecture
    and Director
Center for Architectural Research

School of Architecture
Rensselaer Polytechnic Institute
Troy, New York

HIGHER EDUCATION, Friday, 22 May 1964

PARTICIPANTS

20. Dr. Samuel Baskin
    Director, Program Development
        in Research and Education
    Antioch College
    Yellow Springs, Ohio

21. Dr. Winslow R. Hatch
    Editor
    Division of Higher Education
    U. S. Office of Education
    Washington, D. C.

22. Dr. Alexander Schure
    President,
    New York Institute of Technology
    135-145 West 70th Street
    New York, New York

23. Herbert H. Swinburne, F.A.I.A.
    Nolen, Swinburne and Associates
    1601 Locust Street
    Philadelphia, Pennsylvania

24. Dr. Floyd G. Parker
    Associate Professor
    College of Education
    Michigan State University
    409 Education Building
    East Lansing, Michigan

25. Len Singer
    Director of Learning Resources
    Brandies University
    Waltham, Massachusetts

26. Dr. Roy E. Lieuallen
    Chancellor
    Oregon State System of Higher
        Education
    Eugene, Oregon

27. Dr. Anthony G. Adinolfi
    Director of Planning
    State University Construction Fund
    194 Washington Avenue
    Albany, New York

PROJECT ADVISORY COMMITTEE

28. Dr. Jack V. Edling
    Director, Teaching Research
    Oregon State System of Higher
        Education
    Monmouth, Oregon

29. John Rowlett, A.I.A.
    Caudill, Rowlett, Scott
    Architects, Planners and Engineers
    3636 Richmond Avenue
    Houston 27, Texas

B EDUCATIONAL INNOVATION: AN OVERVIEW

The "innovation explosion" is a very real part of contemporary education; the administrator and policy-maker must contend with it in terms of developing programs, and specifying facilities.

The explosion of innovations has many fine aspects; it is providing educators with new ideas, new techniques, and new materials with which they can provide quality instruction and learning. Of course, not all innovations are significant, sincere, and permanent, but their overall effect on education has been beneficial.

The "innovation explosion" has raised some problems of its own in educational planning:

- Teachers and administrators are so beleagured with choices and variations that many simply avoid the matter altogether; others get confused and make ill-advised decisions.

- Many look on an innovation, or on innovations in general, as promotional gimmicks, as means to bring about false savings, or as means only to keep up with the "educational Joneses."

- Often there is the feeling that it really makes little difference which innovation a district tries as long as it tries one.

- There is widespread opinion that some groups are "buying" change, that is, contributing great sums of money without regard to basic educational values and objectives.

- Often there is genuine concern that the innovation being tried doesn't fit district needs or its educational philosophy.

- Some ideas or approaches are chosen without a complete knowledge of their implications, problems, or even basic conflicts with educational goals. Also, two innovations may be inherently contradictory; both cannot be effectively employed.

- Many a good innovation has been dropped because it was not implemented thoroughly; administrators failed to train or convince staff, only certain segments of the staff became familiar with it, or students were never prepared for it.

- The other extreme from poor implementation can cause problems, too. Getting too "gung-ho" or too involved with mechanics of a specific innovation may cause teachers and administrators to loose sight of its real objectives.

- Combinations of distrust, half-knowledge, poor implementation or over-involvement have often allowed auras of cynicism to build up around an innovation. A classic description of team teaching as "I teach ....you smoke" is typical of this kind of cynicism.

- Less-than-adequate facilities sometimes make it impossible to get a true test of new approaches.

- Means are not built into most innovations for genuine evaluation and reorientation after a period of time; as a result true results are never available to others who want to try the approach.

Some of the results of these problems have been no less than disastrous. Administrators become wary of broaching new ideas; some teachers have been altogether "soured" on innovation in general; and many fine new approaches have been simply disregarded because of poor experiences which are no fault of the innovations themselves. Segments of the educational profession are beginning to see these problems and tackle them through efforts such as:

- Those who feel they have something worthwhile are making sure that administrators and teachers get to see it as objectively as possible; they are beginning to realize that one-sided promotion of good points while glossing over bad ones does more to hurt than to help.

- Expanded, objective coverage of innovations by educational and technical journals is also working to clear away suspicion and doubt.

- More thought is being given to thorough implementation of innovations; detailed preparation and in-service training, special pamphlets and guides, and instructional aids and media to support a new approach may be established before any actual implementation steps are taken.

Several problems remain largely unsolved, though,

- The spirit of competition among schools pushes administrators toward accepting some innovations to keep up with the neighbors and to haphazardly trying to outdo them.

- There is still a need for dissemination of results, both good and bad. It is notable that many grants available today for educational research and demonstration make little or no provision for effectively disseminating the results!

- Schools must still produce clear statements of educational policy and philosophy as yardsticks by which they can measure new ideas and approaches.

- The education of teachers still lags behind the acceptance of new approaches in our schools.

- Teachers are not given assistance and encouragement in change.

- There remains a lack of dynamic educational leadership and the appropriate administrative structures to develop, evaluate, and disseminate innovations.

The importance of this last point should not be underestimated. The answer to the problems caused by the innovation explosion does not lie wholly in dynamic leadership and administrative structures, but many feel that until these are provided, the problem will largely remain.

In a report for the New York State Education Department,* Herbert Brickell suggests what has kept education from finding appropriate ways and means for dealing with innovation: we simply do not understand the innovative process; or if we do, we have failed to translate it into the appropriate leadership patterns and administrative structures. Brickell contends that there are three phases to innovation, and that each requires special people and special atmospheres:

- DESIGN. The actual design of educational innovations requires staff with a particularly high degree of competency — the experienced educator with the appropriate wealth of knowledge and experience in his field — operating in a free, enriched, and almost artificial setting.

- EVALUATION. Accurate evaluation of educational innovations requires another

*H. M. Brickell, Organizing New York State for Educational Change, Albany, The State Education Department, 1961.

kind of person — the professional evaluator, schooled in methods and techniques for testing and analysis — operating in a tightly controlled, observed, an unfree environment.

- DISSEMINATION. Dissemination and demonstration of innovations is a wholly different matter from design and evaluation. This must be done — in order to be convincing — by "typical" teachers in "typical" settings.

Brickell's point is that these three unique aspects of the innovative process are often confused: that designers are put in evaluator roles, dissemination is left in inappropriate hands, and that too many people are required to carry out all three phases by themselves. The problem would be largely solved if educators (1) recognized the distinctness of the phases, (2) placed the proper persons in the proper roles, and (3) created the proper administrative structures.

On the latter point, Brickell suggests first, the creation of a large scale "educational research agency," perhaps one per state (or like the regional education laboratories being proposed under Title IV of the Elementary and Secondary Education Act of 1965). These agencies would sponsor design and evaluation work, and maintain close ties with local units actually responsible for disseminating the innovations. These local units (like the Supplementary Centers proposed under Title III of the same bill) would serve to bring the innovation to the people on a local scale — one center might serve a small group of districts and institutions.

Whether everyone agrees with Brickell or not, it is important that educators and policy-makers on all levels begin to give more attention to the process of innovation. Once the process is better understood, educators can begin to approach innovations with less hesitation and confusion. This clarity can, in turn, manifest itself in better-planned programs and educational facilities.

REPORT **B**

A GUIDE FOR THE DESIGN PROFESSIONS

Library of Congress Catalog Card No. 66-25154
Copyright 1966, Center for Architectural Research, Rensselaer Polytechnic Institute
Photos by Carl Howard and Rensselaer's Offices of Institutional Research and In-
stitute Relations, except pages B-6 and B-60, John Shaver, Architect, Salina, Kansas.

EDUCATIONAL FACILITIES WITH NEW MEDIA
REPORT B: A Guide for the Design Professions

The final report of an architectural research study conducted by the staff of the Center for Architectural Research, School of Architecture, Rensselaer Polytechnic Institute, Troy, New York, under the terms of contract number OE-316-031 between Rensselaer and the United States Office of Education.

Alan C. Green
M. C. Gassman
Wayne F. Koppes
Raymond D. Caravaty
David S. Haviland

CONTENTS

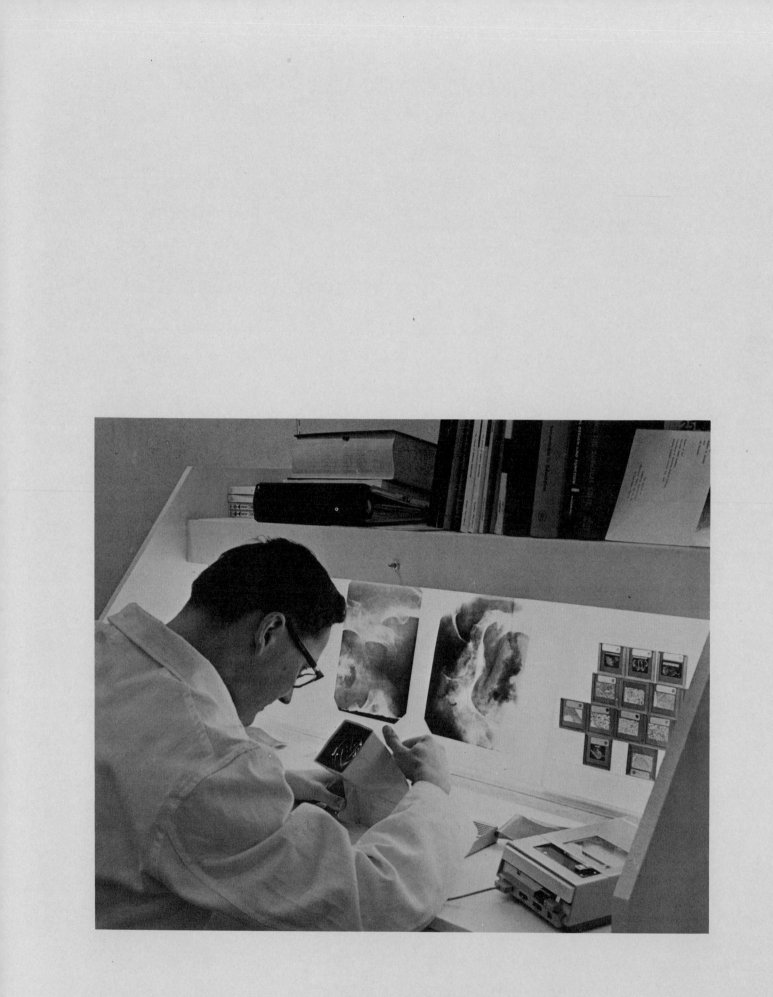

1 LEARNING MEDIA AND FACILITIES: A REVIEW

Innovations indicate impact of media

That learning media are part of the fabric of American education is no longer in doubt. Naturally, not every educator regards media with equal degree of admiration or esteem for what they can do, but none can afford to ignore them. The simple enumeration of innovations in education and the impact of media in each, as presented in Report A of this series, attests to this fact

Media redefined

Learning media were defined in Report A as techniques of varying sophistication utilized for orderly organizing, presenting and storing information and for encouraging appropriate learning responses. Media may be total systems of communication in themselves, or they may serve to aid the communicative process. The printed book is a medium, and so is the chalkboard and the teaching machine.

More media than before

Obviously learning media are nothing new, but the number and variety of media available have increased tremendously over the past decade. It is particularly the newer media—those which have grown out of technological and electronic advances—that most affect the total scope of education and the design of educational facilities.

Uses of media reflect educational concerns...

In review, the development and application of new media has been brought on by a number of concerns responsible for most of the new thinking in education today:

- NUMBERS: our population is growing and a greater percentage of it is going to school; the number of well-qualified teachers and adequate classrooms is not keeping up.

- KNOWLEDGE: our rate of acculumulating knowledge is increasing every day; education must become more generalized and more specialized at the same time.

- SOCIETY: our society is placing greater value on education; not only are better opportunities demanded, but there is national concern for doing so.

- MONEY: our educational machinery keeps growing larger and more complex; to finance this, schools are finding themselves more and more in competition for funds.

...and an explosion of innovations

The result of these concerns has been an explosion of innovations in education; innovations that reflect the directions in quality, efficiency and individualization so prominent in educational thinking today.

---

visual display

    projected------8, 16, 35mm motion pictures
                 slides, 2"x2" to 3 1/4" x 4"
                 film strips
                 overhead transperencies
                 opaque materials
                 shadows of 3-D objects

    non-projected--chalkboard surfaces
                  charts, illustrations, graphics
                  printed materials

audio presentation

    recorded--records and tapes
    telephone
    broadcast radio
    systems for sound distribution

three-dimensional

    models, demonstrations, miniaturized materials

combined audio-video

    sound motion pictures
    sound slides
    printed materials with recorded sound
    kits of audio-video materials

television

    broadcast and closed-circuit
    live and recorded
    reception by monitors, receivers, or projector

programmed instruction

    visual display and texts
    audio presentation
    combined audio-video presentation

information systems

    film-recorded
    computer-based

What learning media can do

The role of learning media in these innovations is a large one. Reasons for this are not hard to uncover,

- Media can make more information available in a variety of forms, and in forms most appropriate to the desired learning situation.

- Media can be used to extend the teacher and the learning situation into areas before untouched.

- Media can make learning more effective by presenting information which is dynamic, emotional, realistic and stimulating and which extends the bounds of traditional methods of instruction.

- Media can make learning more efficient by making more information available to students in shorter times at less expense, using less (but the best) teacher time.

*Media are not
"taking over"*

Learning media are not "taking over" education; teachers will not be replaced by technology. Media can broaden the spectrum of education; they are not total education. They can be used at times, as a substitute for conventional teaching, but are more often used to accomplish learning goals never before possible.

*The future of
hardware*

The future indicates an expanded role for media. There will be more equipment doing more things, and more economically than in the past; specialists in the use of media will be part of the educational team. A goal in hardware development will be compatible, interchangeable components forming systems of equipment for a variety of tasks.

*Implications
of media for...*

However, there are reservations that must be met when using media. During the innovative stages of any new educational process there are pitfalls, misapplications and undesirable results which may obscure the primary objectives behind the innovation. In this light, media makes certain demands on education,

...staff...

- Staff must learn to work and plan together; to be able to define learning objectives, devise systems for teaching, and plan the use of media well in advance of actual needs.

...administration...

- Administrators must provide the educational leadership and climate necessary to carry through innovations.

...planning

- Planners must recognize the impact of media on education and develop facility types that will support and extend their contribution to effective learning.

*Media requires
new concepts
of facilities
and design*

The key word is "planning." Educators must plan for the uses of media in the classroom, and educators and architects together—through the programming process—must specify appropriate facilities for effective use of media. It is this concern with planning and design of facilities to which the remainder of this report is addressed. In fact, the basic premise of this report is that effective utilization of new media requires new concepts in facility types and their design.

2 PLANNING SCHOOLS FOR MEDIA: GENERAL PRINCIPLES

Planning principles reviewed periodically

For the educator-administrator defining building needs and the architect-planner designing schools, the utilization of media implies a number of basic principles for planning that must be considered to assure the creation of an appropriate learning environment. These principles are significant at all stages of the building project; they should first be reviewed when the building is being initially considered, again during detailed programming, and at many points in the actual design and construction. In many cases, the implementation of these principles will not only affect the design and construction of the building itself, but will often require the development of appropriate policy by administrators and boards to insure the successful use of media.

> I don't think there is anything happening today that is more important for us to do than to implement the use of instructional media and aids. It's through these aids and media that we can achieve a higher quality of educational programs. It means new and better instructional materials, better supplies, and more and better equipment.
>
> It means above all, I think, that we are working toward a more precisely controlled environment for learning. And this comes through building design.*
>
> ...Dr. John Gilliland

Principles used by architects, administrators, policy makers

These planning principles are of primary concern to the architect-planner and all others directly involved in design and equipping; they must also be a part of the planning tools of the administrator, and the working vocabulary of the policy maker.

*These quotations are taken from the report of "Three Meetings in May", a series of seminars conducted as part of this project.

2 / PRINCIPLES

*Three categories
of facilities
required*

1. Three general categories of facilities are involved when media are to be properly utilized:

- learning facilities—in which the student or groups of students come together with media for the purpose of learning.

- facilities for storage and access—in which media in various forms are catalogued, stored, and made readily accessible for learning situations.

- production and support facilities—in which media in a variety of forms are produced or originate to meet the needs of particular learning requirements and where the teaching staff receives assistance and support in the effective and efficient use of media.

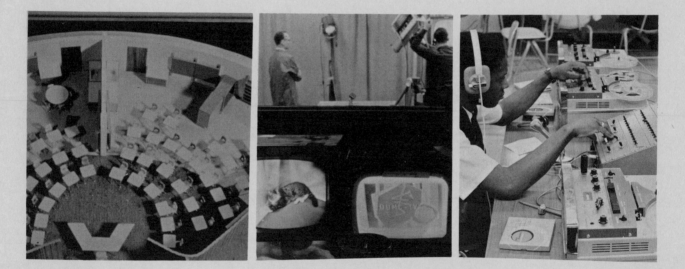

*All types
represented*

For significant uses of new media, all three facility types will be represented; their coordinated planning is an obvious necessity. It is particularly important that these three categories of facilities be first recognized and provided during the programming phase of a school building project.

*Part 3 contains
information on
learning facilities...*

For this report, learning facilities have been divided into six types— independent study; small, medium, large, and flexible groupings; and renovated classrooms. Design studies and information for each type are presented in Part 3.

*...storage and
access facilities...*

Design studies for storage and access, or resource facilities are also presented in Part 3. These spaces may be small and an integral part of the learning spaces, or, with the advent of sophisticated information storage and retrieval systems may include large, centralized electronic storehouses.

...production
and support
facilities

The production and support facilities may house a wide range of functions from teachers making overhead transparencies for classroom use, to television production on a regional basis.

Co-ordinated
systems of
facilities

2. The effective use of media requires the development of systems of facilities composed of elements which represent the three categories of space identified previously. A lecture hall with facilities for using media cannot be considered alone; the media must be produced somewhere and must be made accessible through other types of facilities.

The provision of all the necessary elements to make a total system, and the functional and administrative relationships among the elements must be considered initially during programming, as well as later in planning.

Amen!

> *Our experience has been, that rather than not using multi-purpose rooms enough, we have been trying to use them more than we should. I don't believe basketball and physical education activities and eating should be done in the same place. To borrow an old term, it becomes a "multi-useless" room.*
>
> *...Dr. John Gilliland*

A mix of facility
types seems generally
appropriate

3. For most schools, a mix of these various facility types will be necessary to meet educational objectives. The greatest distinguishing feature among schools should not be the provision of one type of facility with media to the exclusion of others, but an emphasis on one or two types of space within a mix of types. In addition to providing a more stimulating architectural and educational environment, the school with a mix of facilities provides a high degree of flexibility of use and educational approach through the scheduling and utilization of the various facilities.

> *We must realize, however, that no course can meet a student's needs if it is conducted entirely in one size group or in one way, any more than any course can meet a student's total needs if it is done entirely by television.*
>
> *...Dr. Winslow R. Hatch*

*Environment
must not just
house learning*

4. The planning and design of the learning facilities must create an environment which not only houses, but encourages, and in no way interferes with desired learning. This premise has important implications for design features such as lighting, climate, color, seating, acoustics, equipment and controls, and the relating of spaces and circulation. It means that, for instance:

- there should be no glare in a room to distract a viewer's attention.

- seating should not only be comfortable and provide correct posture, but also support other appropriate learning activities —note-taking, referencing, using individual learning materials, etc.

- large expanses of glass admitting natural light may be distracting and may interfere with the display of projected images.

- areas for individual study should not be located near areas of heavy circulation and movement with all the attendent distractions.

It also means that learning objectives must be spelled out before architectural program and plans can be developed.

> Every bit of "noise" you introduce into an environment decreases the ability of the people in it to produce. The more noise of all kinds, the more flickering of light, the more movement that's irrelevant to what you are doing, the more exhausted the people get. There are no exceptions.
>
> ...Dr. Arthur W. Foshay

*Media potentially
available*

5. Appropriate media should potentially available in every learning situation. In some cases, this may simply mean the installation of cables and conduits for future introduction of equipment. Other times, it will necessitate providing for the later incorporation of large information display surfaces and related equipment. This will require initial provision for proper lighting, acoustics, seating and similar design features.

This also requires defining what the potential uses of media in a space may be, before designing space to anticipate its use.

> We need the kinds of teaching and the kinds of facilities that are appropriate to the individual modes and styles of learning that students bring to class. One child can learn well from a recording, from a lecture or from reading; another child learns better from dramatic play, role-playing, or seeing a concrete model or from some other kind of illustration or effort. Each person has his own style, his own way that works best for him and it behooves the school to provide for this range of difference.
>
> ...Dr. Melvin W. Barnes

Often multi-media necessary...

6. Multiple media—media of different types—will be essential in many learning situations. The media must be organized and the facilities planned to permit whatever multiple use is required by learning objectives. For instance, television alone may not be able to carry the full communicative burden in a learning situation; it will be desirable to have films, audio tapes, and other media available for use.

...and sometimes simultaneously

Further, in some situations, two or more types of media will be used simultaneously. Although there is a great deal of research necessary to establish the validity and appropriateness of simultaneous multi-channels of communication, many learning spaces must be designed for the simultaneous display of information.

Interchangeable age levels

7. Facilities for extensive and sophisticated uses of media should be planned to accommodate a range of student maturity levels enabling their reassignment as determined by changing community needs. In view of the costs involved in building and equipping these facilities, they should not be so rigidly geared to one age level that they cannot be assigned for use by other groups as required. This interchange of age levels provides one further type of flexibility in use.

Flexibility has many connotations

8. "Flexibility"—accommodating variations in equipment, teaching methods, technology, and group sizes—is a term with broad and varied implications and with hazards of misunderstanding and misinterpretation. It includes concern for returning to the old as well as changing to accommodate the new. Part 3 devotes a section to design studies which provide flexible groupings. As noted there, flexibility of the kind which calls for demountable and folding partitions can easily place restrictions on effective uses of media through less-than-optimum viewing and hearing conditions.

Four needs in rearranging space

Flexibility to allow rearrangement of space can be defined in terms of four needs:

- hour-to-hour (or even minute-to-minute): the need to accommodate different group sizes, or to provide a variety of learning situations in the school day (or even in the school period). This type of flexibility is best accomplished by moveable panels, space dividers on rollers, folding and accordion partitions. The teachers (and possibly the students) should be able to easily operate whatever devices are used. The whole process of making the change should take no more than a minute or two at most.

- day-to-day: the need to provide for program changes from week-to-week. The same criteria as "hour-to-hour" apply to this type of flexibility, except that there is more time to allow for relocation of heavy furniture and rearranging other contents of the spaces involved.

- term-to-term: the need to accommodate changes in the school schedule—more classes, fewer students, more seminar situations, etc. This is the kind of thing that varies from term-to-term, and there are a few days available to provide the new spaces. Here, demountable partitions are likely to be the answer.

- year-to-year: this is really the same kind of flexibility mentioned in the paragraph above, except that there may be several months in which to provide for it. The traditional answer is knocking down block partitions, rewiring, etc.

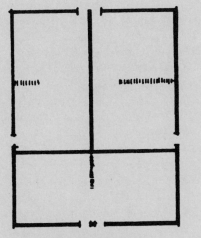

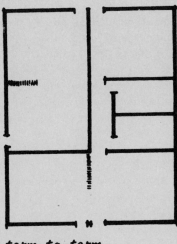

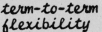

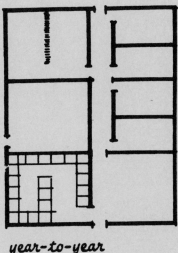

*hour-to-hour &
day-to-day flexibility*

*term-to-term
flexibility*

*year-to-year
flexibility*

**Other types of
flexibility**

As previously mentioned, flexibility may be also achieved by providing a mix of facility types which are scheduled to meet varying needs and by allowing the interchanging of age levels. It may be also achieved by under-utilization of the existing facilities.

**Analyze type of
flexibility by
analyzing functions**

Analyzing learning spaces in terms of functions may help establish the appropriate type of flexibility:

- interchangeable functions: usually small spaces which can be converted from seminar to recitation to individual study, etc. The discipline is not the design standard: the varying functions it houses is. The key is convertability.

- specific functions, but multi-discipline usage: a lecture hall with media supports one educational process or one function; but it can be used by many different disciplines. The scheduling of these spaces provides flexibility.

- specific unidiscipline usage: some learning facilities can only house one function and one discipline; multiple uses are not appropriate.

> *The architect is certainly faced with a real conflict between flexibility in one dimension and commitment in the other. What we're really looking for is some optimal compromise or "trade-off" between these two dimensions.*
>
> *...Dr. John Cogswell*

*Importance of
scheduling*

9. Once group learning spaces permitting extensive use of media are provided, the most efficient means must then be employed for scheduling their use by students, faculty, and courses. Often, this will be computer-based scheduling; it is essential that large, costly facilities with media achieve a high rate of utilization to justify their integral role in a school plant.

*Don't schedule
small spaces
too tight*

However, there is a point where scheduling which is "too tight" will not allow the informal, unplanned learning opportunities that must be encouraged in education, rather than thwarted. Particularly in individual spaces and small group seminar and project rooms, scheduling should not attempt such a high utilization rate that non-scheduled learning is eliminated.

*Plan for change
and updating of
equipment*

10. All facilities which use or which support the use of media should be planned and designed to permit periodic changes of hardware and equipment, as it is impossible to prevent the obsolescence of equipment installed at the time the building is initially occupied. Provisions should be made in anticipation of such eventual changes when the building is designed, and budgeted funds should be available for a long term program of modification and up-dating. Cable-trays, open couduit, and dropped ceilings permit changes in wiring and cables without changing the building itself.

> I think, if the architect and the educator have a joint responsibility here, it is that we can't wait for the matter of equipment to be thought of later; it has to be thought of as part of the building contract. In fact, we don't think of designing space unless we talk about the teaching aids and all the electronic equipment that's needed to do the teaching job.
>
> ...John Shaver, AIA

*Hardware as
systems of
components*

Also, hardware and equipment, the "things" of media, should be considered components of systems which must be co-ordinated to facilitate interchangeability and growth and to help further overcome the problems of obsolescence and change. The use of co-ordinated components can permit economy in initial purchasing, reduction of maintenance and replacement costs, and simplified operation by staff and faculty. Hardware should not be looked on as gimmickry, but as integral elements of the educational process. Only equipment should be included which meets basic economic standards. Often the educational goals can be easily met, by simple, dependable, easily operated, and inexpensive equipment.

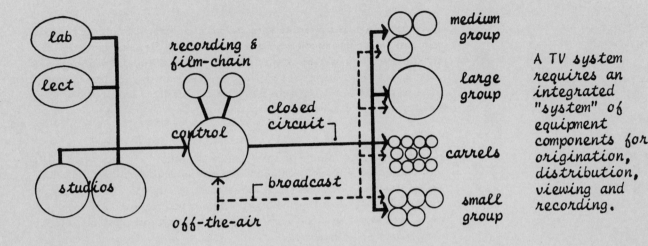

A TV system requires an integrated "system" of equipment components for origination, distribution, viewing and recording.

Remodeling to accommodate media

11. Existing educational facilities should be remodeled to improve their appropriateness for uses of media. Often at a cost much less than new construction, existing facilities can be remodeled for satisfactory use of media. This up-dating process should be a natural and integral part of administrative budgetary planning.

> *I think we've got to also set money aside for making anticipated changes. Are we putting money in budgets, not only to tear down old buildings or to renovate those that are obviously obsolete, but money to make the changes which we know are coming? The building as planned may be perfectly good, but we know we have to make some changes eventually.*
>
> *...Marvin R.A. Johnson, AIA*

Use of a "media module"

The design studies presented in Part 3—"Renovated Classrooms"— are presented specifically to illustrate the effective conversion of existing facilities. Often minimum expense is involved once a "media module" or some other form of an "equipment-cabinet unit" has been provided. (see study SG-1 in Part 3). The conversion of existing facilities calls for great ingenuity and creativeness on the part of the designer, but can easily become the most significant investment a school can make.

Use of media for other types of education

12. Educational facilities with media are capable of rendering service far beyond the normal school day and should be planned to include programs such as continuing education, job retraining, cultural enrichment, and adult education. Experimental uses of media in such programs have indicated an expanded role for media in all types of educational activities; certainly, such uses should be considered early in the programming phase.

*Location
becomes
important*

When facilities are to serve extra-school day functions, their position within the school plant becomes important. Design of entrances, circulation and parking; ease of control and security; and relationship among facilities such as lockers, resources and supplies, all guide the problem of location within the plant.

*Regional
cooperation in
uses of media*

13. In planning, consideration should be given to providing facilities for regional cooperative programs in the origination, production, and dissemination of instructional resources. Each school does not print its own textbooks; neither can each school or district produce all the necessary instructional materials. Experimental programs in several locations throughout the country today are indicating the logic, if not the necessity, of such regional production facilities.

*Regionalization
implies new
building types*

The impact of such regional approaches is indicated by the discussion of new building types in Part 3. Further, recent Federal legislation (Titles II and III of the Act of 1965) underscores the significance of regionalization by providing funds for implementing programs including production and evaluation of media.

*Facilities with
media important
in innovations*

14. The planning of educational facilities with media, particularly the conversion of existing facilities, can play a significant role in encouraging educational change towards realistic, well-defined goals. Innovations in education can be directed and encouraged by the kinds of facilities provided, and certainly, facilities which permit the use of media are among the most significant. Emphasis should be placed on the small, local, inexpensive demonstration project which brings innovations—and proper facilities—to the local teacher and professor.

*Planning for
visitors*

There is another side to innovation and facilities. Schools designed to house particular innovations will certainly attract large numbers of visitors. Provision should be made for handling these visitors, for observing without disturbing, when the school is initially designed.

*Facilities for
teachers and
professors*

15. Planning for appropriate uses of media requires facilities for teachers and professors, facilities such as offices, planning and conference rooms, reference and resource areas, and simple teacher-oriented production. These facilities will be scattered about the educational plant with many of them oriented to the library or resource center.

*Faculty trained
to use facilities
properly*

16. Providing all the necessary facilities for utilization of media does not guarantee that the facilities will be used effectively. Administrative leadership must assure that production and resource facilities are properly staffed and that the staff is motivated to assisting teachers and professors in meeting instructional objectives. In addition, training programs, in-service education, release-time for planning and other procedures must be employed to ready and to train the faculty in the proper use of facilities with media.

> In my opinion, before you have a good faculty, you must have a good backup staff in terms of technicians, assistants, and multi-media people. After this, you need the properly motivated faculty.
>
> ...Herbert H. Swinburne, FAIA

*Detailed design
criteria required
in planning
specific rooms*

Finally, the planning of individual spaces and rooms for the use of media, or to support their use, requires special attention to design criteria such as the location of display surfaces, the definition of viewing areas, the planning of lighting, seating, and acoustics, the arrangement of entrances and circulation paths, and the positioning of equipment, conduit, and controls. Specific design criteria are discussed in terms of individual facility types in Part 3. Detailed design information is presented in Report C—A Technical Guide," and is summarized in Part 4 of this Report B.

3 FACILITIES WITH MEDIA: PLANNING GUIDANCE

*Design guidance
for facility types*

The general principles for planning schools with media discussed in Part 2 will eventually be translated into physical form through the design of the various parts of schools and colleges—classrooms, lecture halls, seminar rooms, laboratories, resource centers, production-support areas, and so on. Each of these facility types, using or supporting the use of media, requires special consideration. Guidance in their design seems especially appropriate and useful at this time.

*Nine categories
of facilities
in this part*

The facility types to be presented in this Part 3 are organized into nine categories; the first six deal with learning spaces according to size, grouping and appropriateness for renovation. The seventh and eighth cover the other elements of the "media system"—resource and production-support facilities. The last category presents three new building types which have resulted from the utilization of media.

*Stock solutions
inappropriate*

Therefore, in this Part, the text and graphics describe facility types rather than total school buildings. This is intentional. Since the way in which these facility types are chosen and put together will vary according to individual needs and philosophies, it would be presumptuous and unrealistic to offer total or stock solutions.

*Graphics show
principles, not
"pat solutions"*

It is assumed that once the programming process has established the kinds of facilities required, the designer-planer will turn to the appropriate pages in this Part for guidance in design. The graphics are not to be taken as "pat solutions" to be copied for ready use; they are presented because graphics seem the best way to communicate with designers.

IS INDEPENDENT STUDY FACILITIES

Probably no concept has sparked more attention or caused more debate than that of independent study and its role in contemporary education. As more schools and colleges provide for more individualization, as more students are encouraged to assume responsibility for their own learning, and as a wider variety of experiences are introduced into education, the need for housing independent study becomes an important planning factor.

Even the strongest proponents of independent study do not agree on how much time the student should spend working on his own. Those who have studied the situation, however, agree on some basic points:

- No student will spend all his time in independent study, and not all students can handle independence. There are wide variations.

- Independent study needs to be complemented by group activities, particularly seminar and project situations which allow a small group to share experiences.

- Programs utilizing a high degree of independent study place special demands on the teacher, support staff, administration, resources and facilities. Certainly independent study programs are not undertaken to reduce the need for these things.

Implications for facilities to accommodate independent work remain somewhat indefinite; they will vary widely, according to particular philosophy and way in which it is implemented. To complicate this, educators and architects are continually impressed with how little they really know about the learning environment and how it can add to or detract from effective learning. Questions such as, "How isolated should the student be?", "Should he stay put or be allowed to move around constantly?", "Does he need a visual contact with the out-of-doors?", "How much control should he have over his environment?" are being asked for all levels of education. So far there are not many definitive answers.

Despite these obstacles, there are certain points that can be made about independent study facilities:

Spaces for Independent Study

- No single room in the school building should be set aside as an independent study room; these areas are best scattered throughout the building to be where the students are.

- Areas for independent study can be set aside in many places of school buildings —both new and existing. Diagram A illustrates this point.

- Independent study units probably function best if grouped in small clusters. In this way they can share common services and other elements of environment such as lighting, acoustics and climate control.

	existing buildings	new buildings
project areas	- as project rooms or areas within remodeled facilities - EXAMPLE: RC-7	- as project rooms or areas associated with a variety of different spaces and groups of spaces - EXAMPLES: SG-6, MG-2, MG-4, LG-4, LG-5
classrooms	- within existing classrooms - in former cloakrooms and other spaces between existing classrooms - EXAMPLES: RC-2, RC-3	- within new classrooms - between new classrooms - as part of a suite of facilities including classrooms - should be in view of teacher in elementary schools; some isolation is permissible in secondary schools - EXAMPLES: MG-1, MG-3, MG-4, LG-5, FG-1, FG-2, FG-3
resources centers	- limitations due to lack of conduit for electronic carrels and insufficient electrical outlets for projection devices, recorders, etc. - general lack of room for carrels - inadequate lighting a problem	- relate to media storage - avoid regimented appearance - may be scatted throughout stack and reference areas - may be related to both classrooms and resources center - EXAMPLES: RF-1, RF-2, RF-3
cafeteria, gymnasiums, etc.	- simple carrels can be created by portable dividers used with dining tables - difficult to introduce electronic devices - problems of light, ventilation, circulation and regimentation	- can use furniture with built-in outlets & plug-in electrical and TV conduits - portable equipment with built-in or portable dividers on dining tables - problems of light, circulation, and sound
circulation areas	- probably prohibited by codes, lack of adequate space, and insufficient lighting	- may work if circulation is not distracting and if light and acoustical control is possible - may work as "cul-de-sac" spaces just off circulation areas

DIAGRAM A

There may be larger groupings in and around the resources or instructional materials center. Particularly in the lower grades, independent study areas will be related directly to the group learning spaces.

- If many study units (such as carrels) are brought together, it is important to visually and functionally "break-up" the space in which they are situated. Students have always shown a marked dislike for studying in large barn-like spaces filled with other students and regimented furniture.

- Placing study units in or adjacent to corridors or circulation spaces may add noise problems and the distraction of moving people.

Relating Independent Study to other Facilities

- Project and seminar areas where students can get together and share learning experiences should be adjacent to independent study areas.

- Particularly in the lower grades, independent study areas should be directly related to group rooms. In upper levels, the independent areas will be related to discipline-oriented facilities, as well.

- In schools relying heavily on an independent study concept, spaces for teachers should be close to the independent study areas in order to allow for consultation, conference sessions, and other close student-teacher contact.

- If students are to remain in individual learning experiences for long periods of time, nearby "social" or "commons" areas for interaction and relaxing may be desirable.

- Evaluation and testing spaces will be needed if continuous progress or non-grading is part of the school's program.

- Some (maybe many) independent study units should have access to the resource center; this may be done by locating them in or near the center, or by using remote "call-up" devices to bring the resources to the student. As the technology moves ahead, the latter will become an increasingly desirable way to solve the problem.

- Many of these relationships among facilities are illustrated by Diagram B.

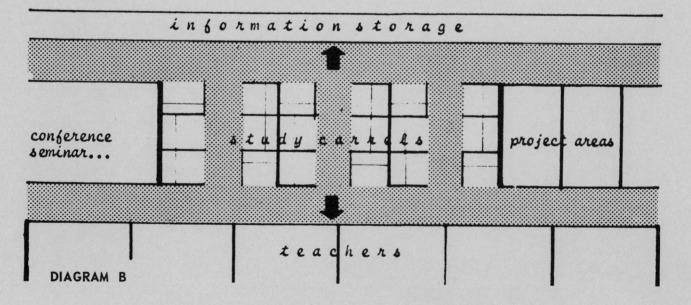

DIAGRAM B

Independent Study Units

- The actual study unit may be an enclosed or semi-enclosed carrel, with or without electronic devices which can be commercially bought or "home-built" and sometimes it can accommodate more than one student. Study units may also include cubicles, enclosed rooms, special equipment and seat units, tables and chairs, lounge chairs, built-in seating, or any other unit which provides the particular functions a student needs to work, study, and learn by himself.

- Carrel units may either be assigned to students as a "home-base", or be available on a "first come—first served" basis. The former approach is appropriate in schools which abandon homerooms in favor of the "home-base" concept.

- Some carrels may accommodate special functions such as typing, teaching machines, audio-visual call-up, audio recording, and computer-based learning. It might be wise to group units according to special types to minimize interference between them.

- Special-purpose carrels may require wiring, gas, water, or air service. Most study carrels will not need these services, except for power outlets.

- With individual carrel units, storage space for books and materials (possibly coats, hats) is necessary. Even if carrels are not assigned to specific students, thought should be given to providing spaces for keeping books and materials in the unit on a "reserve" basis.

- Carrels will vary in design; some should give students a sense of privacy and "identity" but not complete isolation, while others will provide total acoustic and visual privacy. Individual units, particularly carrels, will vary in design and function depending on the age level, the duration of occupancy, and the learning functions to be housed.

- As a general rule, no one type of study unit should be provided exclusively. A mix of many different types, functions, and groupings will usually best meet a school or college's programs. In any case, row upon row of carrels, all exactly the same, should be avoided.

Environmental Concerns

- Adequate lighting is a must. Overall illumination should be soft with particular emphasis given to the working surfaces. Glare should be avoided. The details of lighting in terms of quality and quantity will vary according to the individual's task.

- Acoustic considerations vary according to the functions and type of independent unit. A wide range of allowable noise levels can be found between different independent study areas. Typing, audio recording, and uses of recorded sound should be isolated from other independent functions, although head-phone sets are alleviating the latter problem.

- Students in independent study should be free from distractions of sound, movement, light and climatic changes. In other words, design out ringing telephones, glare, drafts, unrelated circulation, and such.

- Ventilation must be carefully designed; air change should be frequent and some thought might be given to some variations in temperatures to allow for some individual preferences.

- In colleges, if smoking is permitted in the school building, some independent study units should be in restricted areas.

The applications of some of these principles are included in the material on "Resource Facilities". Whenever the independent study units are provided—in classroom, resources center, study area, laboratory, or wherever—they should be designed and arranged to accommodate a variety of functions. This will usually be accomplished by a mix of types of units. Educators have decried the use of "self-contained classrooms" to solve educational needs; careful planning and design will be necessary to prevent the "self-contained classroom" from being replaced by the "self-contained carrel".

SG SMALL-GROUP FACILITIES

Small—group instruction is no longer the prerogative of higher education. Many innovations in elementary and secondary education, particularly nongradedness, tracking and various forms of team teaching and planning, have rendered seminar rooms, project rooms, and student conference facilities not only desirable, but often necessary as part of the system to carry out educational objectives. The provision of media in these rooms, both as part of a larger communication system and for self-contained uses, is a significant refinement that is finding more and more educational acceptance.

In general, small group spaces provided with media may be:

- Part of a resource center to be used by groups of students with and without teachers to review and to learn from resource materials such as films, slides, and transparencies. Such small group spaces may be nonscheduled and used informally and on demand, or they may be a scheduled part of a course or curriculum.

- Part of a teachers' area when informal and nonscheduled conferences and seminars are encouraged, particularly in nongraded and individualized programs. Such a teachers' area may contain a number of teachers' offices plus the small-group spaces, or the small-group spaces may double as teachers' offices.

- Scattered about higher, secondary, or middle school buildings, both as sched-

uled and informal use spaces. These will often occur in conjunction with laboratories, large group classrooms, and specialized instructional rooms where it is desirable to take a part of a group aside for special small group activities, or where a large group is quickly divided into several smaller groups for interactive and more personal learning.

- Grouped together and scheduled as multi-discipline spaces, particularly in higher and secondary education. Here the seminar or conference is as much a part of the instructional techniques as recitation, laboratory, and lecture. Groups of seminar rooms must be provided as are classrooms, laboratories, and lecture halls.

The provision of media creates no great design problems when planning new schools or remodeling existing ones, once the uses of media with small groups have been determined. There are some planning considerations which should be kept in mind as programming and design proceed:

- A variety of seating arrangements—tables, loose chairs, and table—chair units—are possible as long as all seats fall within the viewing area or any significant display surface or combination of display surfaces.

- There is a variety of small, lightweight, and relatively inexpensive projectors—slide, film, and overhead—that work well in small rooms since high lumen output and elaborate remote control features are not important. Particularly significant is the development of 8mm film projectors, including the cartridge-loaded type, for use in rooms of this type.

- With small images of high brightness and often with little or no outside natural light to control, either front or rear projection may be used. In this type of room, white plaster walls can be used for front projection, or self-contained cabinets—"media modules"—can be built in (or used as moveable elements) within the room.

- For most rooms of this size, a single 23" or 24" TV receiver or monitor will provide good viewing for all occupants.

- Lighting is generally easily handled; either incadescent or fluorescent systems will work satisfactorily. Two levels of illumination would be highly desirable; the lower level would be used during projection.

- A character conducive to informality and interchange can easily be introduced in this type of room through the use of carpeting; the careful selection of furniture textures and colors; the design and detailing of the room, and the room's own inherently small scale.

In view of the current concern for achieving high utilization rates for educational facilities, it should be cautioned that much of the benefit of the conference and seminar can be lost if the spaces are scheduled too tightly. Slack in the scheduling of this kind of space is important to encourage informal and student-initiated learning experiences by class changes and prescheduled uses.

SMALL-GROUP STUDY SG-1

Planners of educational facilities are often struck by the similarity between small group learning activities and the kinds of discussion and interaction that take place around the table in a dining room or restaurant. The concentration and focus of the individuals around the table, whether eating or learning, seem to exclude the noise and distraction caused by others in the room similarly engaged.

This study explores the possibility of utilizing dining facilities for seminar and conference activities. Here the utilization of media is handled by cabinets containing equipment which are opened up and around which the group focuses its attention. The cabinet provides a projection screen for a small overhead projector located on the table, a rear projection screen for films and slides, and chalkboard and tackboard surfaces. Four groupings could be located around a core of four such cabinets.

These cabinets could be permanently located in the dining room and opened up during the normal academic day for discussions, seminars, and conferences. The plan indicates the location of several such media centers and the groups that they would serve. As an alternate approach, the cabinets could be mobile and brought into the dining area and positioned as needed for instruction. A further refinement would be fixed cabinets with mobile equipment carts which would permit the interchanging of various types of equipment.

Recorded sound accompanying any of the projected media would be handled by individual head sets or low volume speakers mounted on the folding wings and directed to serve only the small group gathered near the cabinet.

It has often been assumed that cafeterias and dining halls should be used for large group instruction in order to increase the utilization of such facilities. It may well be that a better answer is to use such space for small group activities which can also utilize learning media.

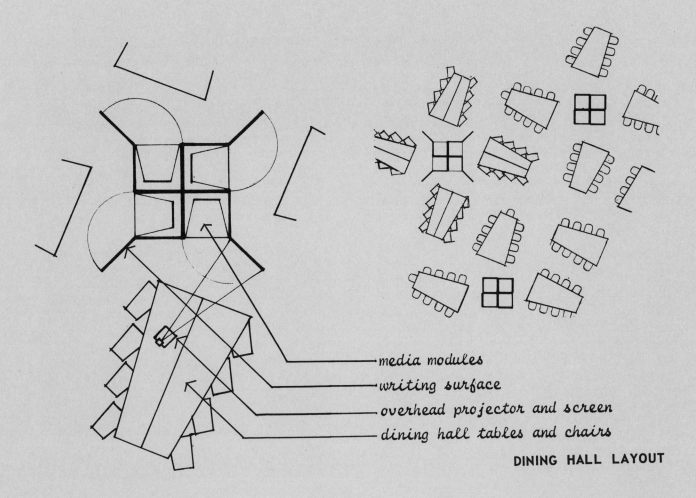

media modules
writing surface
overhead projector and screen
dining hall tables and chairs

DINING HALL LAYOUT

This study led to the design and development of a self-contained media cabinet which might be used in many types of small and medium group situations. These "media modules" can be of several types:

- a fixed cabinet with self-contained equipment, rear projection screen and several additional "swing-out" display surfaces.

- same as above, only the entire media module would be mobile.

- a basic fixed cabinet with rear projection screen and "swing-out" display surfaces. Projection equipment would be mounted on mobile carts which would roll into the cabinet and which would permit the interchanging of projectors.

- same as above with both the basic cabinet and the equipment carts mobile.

- any of the above, but with a cabinet and rear projection screen sized to accommodate two rear projected images side-by-side.

Media modules have several attractive features. They can be fabricated in a shop and installed in existing classrooms with little disruption of normal class meetings; in this way, media modules can quickly and inexpensively convert existing facilities for uses of media. Both in building new facilities and remodelling old, the media module is a relatively inexpensive answer initially, which also readily adapts to new and improved equipment. Mobile units can be designed for flexible spaces where regrouping students frequently is an important functional requirement; fixed installations of media might not be feasible in such circumstances. As illustrated in this study, media modules can be used to increase the utilization of facilities such as dining rooms and gymnasiums by also allowing them to be used for instruction.

The accompanying drawings and photographs illustrate one type of media module which was designed and built as part of this project. The basic cabinet with screen and display surfaces could be either fixed or mobile. Various types of projectors can be mounted in the cart which is rolled into position for projection on the rear projection screen. Remote controls operate the equipment and the rear screen is of the flexible type. This media module has a screen surface 32 inches square and the entire unit stands 6'-8" high. Naturally, these dimensions will vary from module to module.

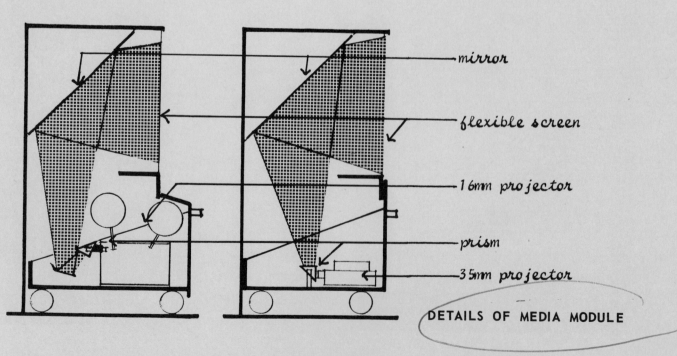

mirror

flexible screen

16mm projector

prism

35mm projector

DETAILS OF MEDIA MODULE

SMALL-GROUP STUDY SG-2

Wedge-shaped spaces can work well as conference and seminar rooms, and can also lend themselves to groupings for economy of space and circulation. Here three rooms, each based on an equilateral triangle and each planned with double access, a media module for slides or films, and an overhead projector are shown with different seating arrangements. In one, chairs can be grouped in circles or semi-circles, with the tables against the wall. For more formal presentations, chairs and tables can be arranged in rows facing the apex or media module. Finally, the tables and chairs can be put together in typical conference form. In any case, the seating occurs within the appropriate viewing area for the screens; the screens would have the characteristics of narrow viewing angle and high gain.

When several such rooms are clustered together, an equipment and service core is created. Media modules can be built-in or temporarily set in this core, utilizing common wiring and power service.

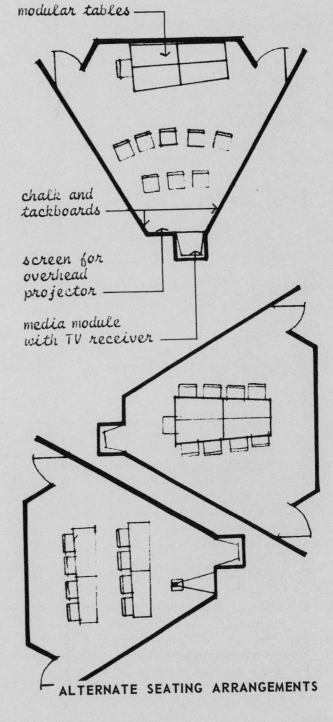

modular tables

chalk and tackboards

screen for overhead projector

media module with TV receiver

ALTERNATE SEATING ARRANGEMENTS

Groupings of rooms such as these would work well for seminars and conferences at the secondary and higher levels of education, and could also serve as project rooms. As elementary education programs move into nongradedness, some rooms of this type will find their way into the elementary school. Also, in a cluster of rooms of this type, one or two might be designated as teachers rooms or offices—probably with double occupancy—creating a "teacher office and seminar center."

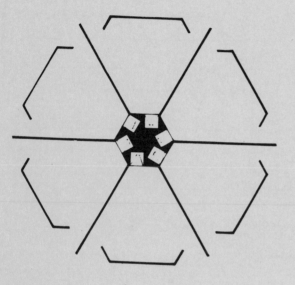

PLAN

MODEL

SMALL-GROUP STUDY SG-3

When more extensive uses are made of media, and when multiple ways of displaying information are desired, the small group room will take on a more rectangualr shape. Here, three plans indicate a basic square room with the media and display surfaces organized in one corner, toward which students will be focused. In this relatively small room, the arrangement will allow for a TV receiver, two media modules or screen surfaces, a front projected overhead projector, and chalk and tackboard surfaces, all of which fall within the appropriate viewing area. The different seating arrangements include modular tables and chairs for rearrangement possibilities, and the horseshoe-shaped fixed counters with loose seats. The small plan and model show how such seminar rooms can be grouped together. Obviously, this basic plan is very adaptable to renovated and remodeled space. It shows that a corner orientation can make a square room appropriate for media, and economical of space.

In these schemes, the pieces of equipment may be either fixed in place as built-in furniture or may be mobile units which can be moved from room to room and rearranged as the instructional situation demands.

This type of room seems most appropriate at the secondary and college level, and would likely be provided in banks or rooms loosely scheduled to allow "slack" for informal learning situations.

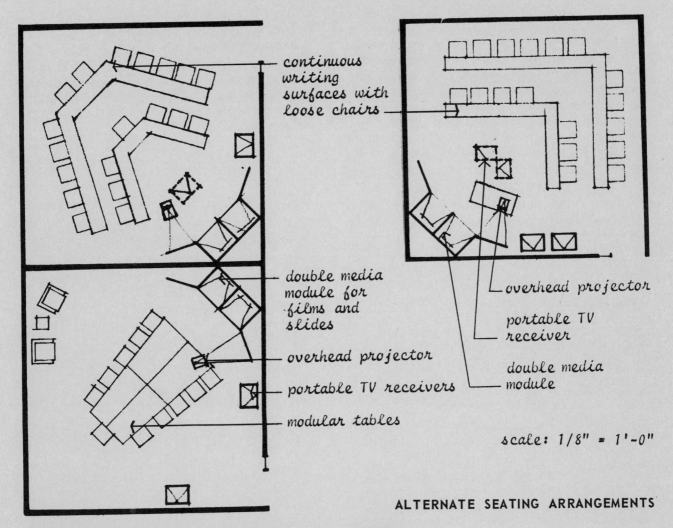

continuous writing surfaces with loose chairs

double media module for films and slides

overhead projector

portable TV receivers

modular tables

overhead projector

portable TV receiver

double media module

scale: 1/8" = 1'-0"

ALTERNATE SEATING ARRANGEMENTS

GROUP ARRANGEMENT

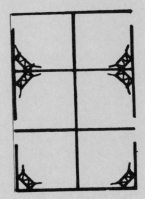

SMALL-GROUP STUDY SG-4

School teachers, even more than school students, need a place to call their own—an office, a work area, or least an individual cubicle. With the classroom becoming less and less used as the teachers' office, provision must be made for her somewhere else. Incorporation of teachers' offices are discussed in several places throughout the design studies. Here, the teacher's office also becomes a small-group conference and seminar room,—or a studio. This kind of room would be most appropriate in some kinds of nongraded curriculam where spontaneous conferences are encouraged, or where the educational program involves a great deal of counselling, personal guidance, and individual attention.

This teacher's office and small-group room is equipped with a media module for films, slides, and overhead projector. In addition, there are opportunities for chalkboard and tackboard surfaces in addition to the teacher's desk, filing cabinets, and coat space. In some instances, such an office could well accommodate two teachers, or a teacher and a teacher's assistant. This type of space, in addition to its applications at the secondary level, would offer a great deal of promise to the college and university designed to reintroduce personal contact between student and faculty.

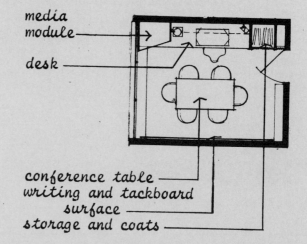

media
module
desk
conference table
writing and tackboard
surface
storage and coats

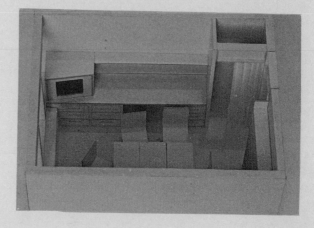

SMALL-GROUP STUDY SG-5

Another way to handle teachers' office space and small-group facilities is expressed by this scheme which places a series of teachers' cubicles or home bases around a small-group instructional space which can also be used for conferences. In this setting, the teacher is provided with basically a private space where she work, correct papers, prepare lessons, etc. When the time comes for conferences and small group teaching activities, she moves from her cubicle to a directly accessible, small-group room designed for those purposes. The small-group room contains modular tables with chairs that will form a variety of arrangements, focused on a series of information display surfaces.

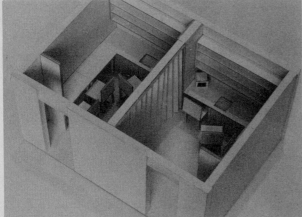

This type of space would also become the planning center for the team of teachers who occupy the cubicles surrounding the conference center. Thus, the small-group room becomes not only a teaching space, but a teacher's planning room. Such a suite of rooms could be assigned to each team within an elementary or secondary school plant. Further, if mobile equipment is used in the conference room, it will be possible to move the equipment on occasion to one of the teacher's cubicles for her own use in previewing and preparing class materials. Also, each teacher's cubicle would be provided with a TV receiver for monitoring off-the-air programs, and for other communication needs.

PLAN

scale: 1/8" = 1'-0"

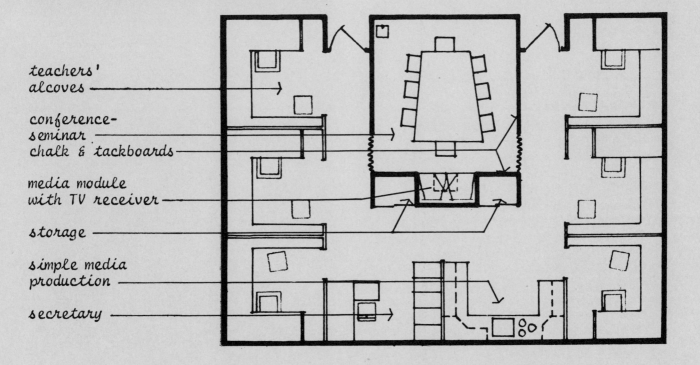

teachers' alcoves

conference-seminar chalk & tackboards

media module with TV receiver

storage

simple media production

secretary

SMALL-GROUP STUDY SG-6

In middle and secondary school programs, and particularly those geared to independent study, there arises a need for individual and small-group project rooms. These rooms, equipped with sink, services, and work space, and designed for the use of media are often employed in physical and natural science courses for independent and small group projects. The room permits a student or small group of students to conduct a project or series of projects over a period of time; work does not have to be terminated by the ring of the bell at the end of a class period. Such project rooms would normally be related to the appropriate laboratory facilities with storage and preparation rooms providing equipment and supplies. However, they could also be part of a resource center if the means of servicing them is available.

This study shows how two small project rooms may act independently for a group of no more than three students each, or how they may be opened together for small group activities involving six to eight. This degree of flexibility is certainly desirable in rooms of this size and function.

As a small project room, information display is handled either by TV receivers or by portable equipment with images being projected on the white plaster projection wall. When the partition is open, the modular tables are pulled away from the wall and, with the loose chairs, may be set up in a number of different ways. In the upper plan, the horseshoe arrangement will allow two images to be projected simultaneously on the projection wall and they can be used in conjunction with the TV monitor. In the lower plan, a larger image may be projected on a pull-down screen at the far end, and the remaining wall space becomes a writing surface. Of course, with the tables pushed back against the wall and the partition opened, a group of six to eight students all involved in the same type of project may occupy the room. The tables against the wall become additional work surfaces.

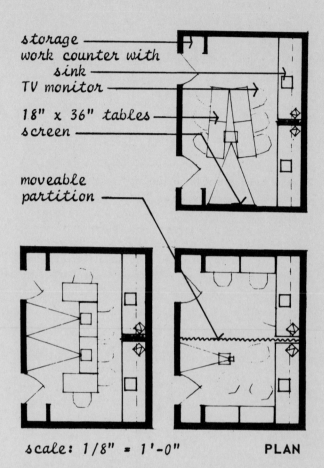

storage

work counter with sink

TV monitor

18" x 36" tables

screen

moveable partition

scale: 1/8" = 1'-0"   PLAN

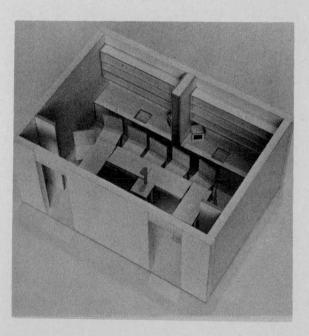

MG MEDIUM-GROUP FACILITIES

25-40 students

Even though the role of the medium size or conventional classroom has been diminished by many of the innovations in contemporary education, it is certainly logical to assume that rooms seating from 25 to 40 will continue to be needed and built. These design studies illustrate the basic design and planning considerations for rooms housing recitation and other medium-group activities.

In general, design and planning of medium-group facilities involves no complicated planning problems. Generally, basic tenets of viewing must be followed, but this usually involves simply arranging seating inside the viewing area defined by the size and location of projection surfaces. If, because of the seating type or complexities of furniture and equipment, sight lines become critical, then stepped flooring will be necessary (as in design studies MG–2 and MG–3). Otherwise, flat floors and simple ceiling configurations are quite satisfactory.

The general shape of the medium-group room is often a square or variations on it, either focused to a corner or focused to one side; in the latter case, the front corners become storage, preparation, or other adjunct facilities. Several different

---

*Details of the media module are presented in design study SG–1.

types and combinations of lighting systems will provide the two or three levels of light required, depending on the number and types of display systems being used. Generally, rear projection has been selected for these rooms, utilizing either a media module or a rear projection area.* The overhead projector is used on fixed or "swing-out" projection surfaces, which may also double as tackboard and chalkboard surfaces. Media modules may be either fixed or mobile, depending on the utilization of media within the room.

Furniture and equipment pose no special problems. With the wide variety in school furniture available, it is only up to the imagination of the architect and the resources of the school to make appropriate decisions.

Some studies in this group, and elsewhere in Part 3, are noted as appropriate for elementary and pre-school education. Here the size of the room will vary significantly based on the number of children, the learning methods involved, and any supplementary equipment required. Particularly in kindergarten and other pre-school programs, the square footage per student will be larger than necessary in typical elementary grades.

The four schemes that follow illustrate a recitation room; a lecture-laboratory for sciences; an audio laboratory for languages, drama, speech, and other communicative skills; and a multi-class room for the simultaneous teaching of groups in several related discipline areas.

MEDIUM-GROUP STUDY MG-1

The basic point illustrated by this scheme is that a square room is the optimum shape for medium-group spaces. The 30—odd seats are oriented to a variety of display surfaces and types of media located in one corner of the room. This orientation, in a square room, best encloses an optimum viewing area as shown in the plan by the arrangement of the seats. Around the periphery of the room are located project areas, coat area, independent study stations, and supplementary display surfaces. By using the media module, windows on the one wall may be as extensive or limited as desired, although draperies or shades will be required behind the media area to prevent glare in the face of the viewers.

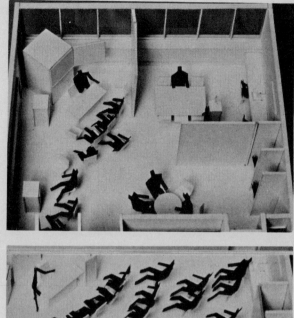

The other plan and model indicate how the room can be quickly reorganized into a series of small-group and independent study activities. The loose tables and chairs are reoriented in seminar fashion; one or two groups may use the media modules and TV monitors. In all groups, the use of the overhead projector is made possible by the media module screens and the swing-out space dividers.

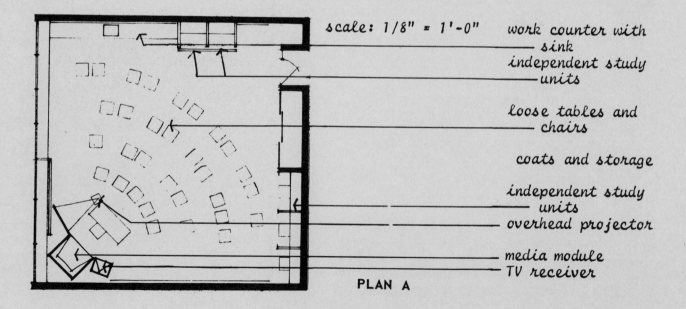

scale: 1/8" = 1'-0"

work counter with sink

independent study units

loose tables and chairs

coats and storage

independent study units

overhead projector

media module

TV receiver

PLAN A

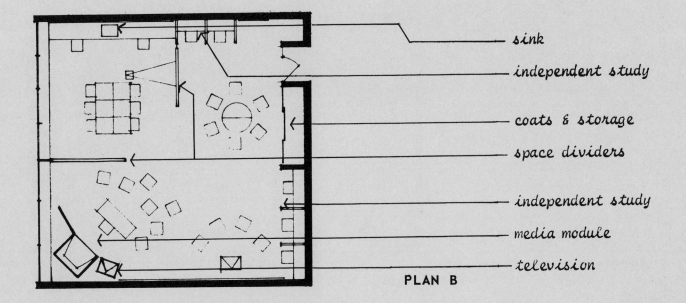

sink

independent study

coats & storage

space dividers

independent study

media module

television

PLAN B

MEDIUM-GROUP STUDY MG-2

This is a medium-group science room, which by simple modification of the equipment and services can be used for both natural and physical sciences. The basic premise of the room is that the presentation phases and laboratory phases of a learning experience in science do not need to take place in separate facilities, but rather that by proper design of the room and proper provision of equipment both functions may take place interchangeably and sometimes concurrently.

This scheme shows a central core of facilities serving two science rooms "back-to-back." The central core contains preparation and projection spaces for each classroom, as well as project rooms. The front of the room contains a demonstration table which is backed by projection screens, a media module and supplementary display surfaces. Reagents and other supplies for student use are prepared and distributed

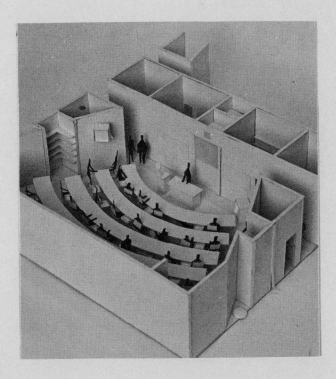

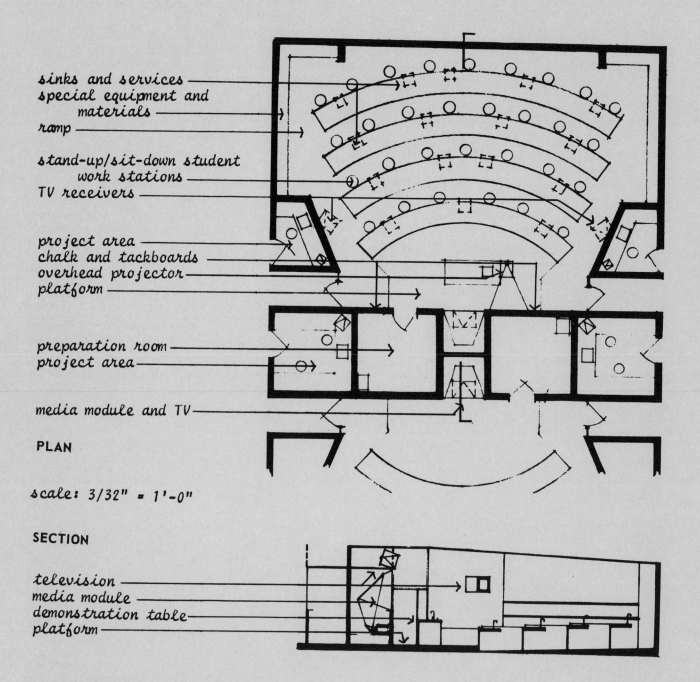

sinks and services
special equipment and
materials
ramp

stand-up/sit-down student
work stations
TV receivers

project area
chalk and tackboards
overhead projector
platform

preparation room
project area

media module and TV

PLAN

scale: 3/32" = 1'-0"

SECTION

television
media module
demonstration table
platform

from the preparation room by mobile carts moving up the ramped aisles. The student work station is composed of a large work surface, with sink and utilities serving every two students. The student has an option, as shown in the section, of either standing to work or sitting at the bench.

Although the square foot per student area in a room of this type is excessive when compared to conventional lecture rooms, the ability to save laboratory space by combining functions is both economically and educationally justified.

The project rooms, which may be used by one or two students are provided for long term special projects and for advanced students. They may or may not be used by students who are a part of the group occupying the main part of the room.

MEDIUM-GROUP STUDY MG-3

There seems to be little reason for creating rooms used solely for the teaching of languages. In essence, the so-called "language laboratory" is really an audio room which should be available for those aspects of drama, speech, history, music, as well as languages, which adapt themselves to audio presentation. Further, such activities may require some variations in group sizes, depending upon the instructional methods and organizational patterns. This scheme presents the concepts for a medium-group audio laboratory, plus an individual study area and small-group room. The audio system for all three types of space can be controlled from the teacher's control station.

The 30—odd audio stations are grouped on a stepped floor and oriented to display surfaces for those times when audio and video information are used in conjunction with each other. The individual audio carrels, the small-group room, and the teacher's control station are located in the spaces occuring between the medium-group rooms when several are located side-by-side. The scheme shows development of an audio suite which allows the teachers to move freely through it from the control center.

The student stations in this laboratory could sometimes be considered as individual learning stations. Then, programmed instruction utilizing "machines" could be used at each station, or each station could feed into a central computer facility for computer-based individual learning.

PLAN

scale: 3/32" = 1'-0"

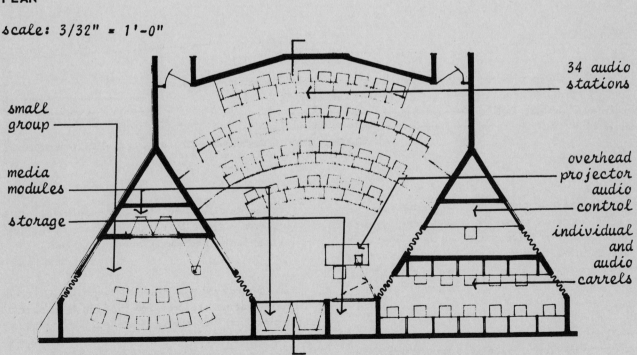

small group

media modules

storage

34 audio stations

overhead projector audio control

individual and audio carrels

SECTION

The plan and section, and the photograph of the model, indicate the circulation pattern and the arrangement of furniture and equipment within the suite. The detail of the seating arrangement indicates that the lowering of the divider panel between student stations permits the group to function together, and may even encourage some interaction if it becomes appropriate.

Audio received in this room may be distributed from a number of sources—a central library, a central tape bank, remote locations away from the school, or tape decks within the suite. All of these possibilities should be considered and provided for in the selection and installation of the audio equipment and control system.

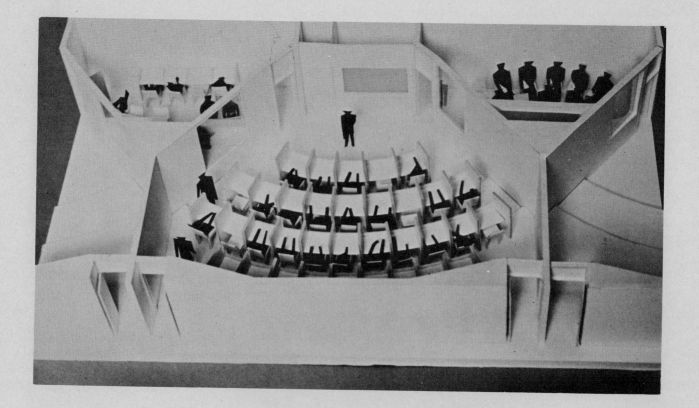

MEDIUM-GROUP STUDY MG-4

In many small secondary schools and colleges, student enrollments are not large enough to permit the offering of separate sections in a variety of related courses. For this reason, multi-class teaching has begun to play a significant role, and appropriate facilities for multi-class teaching are being considered. This design study presents a multi-class science suite utilizing a variety of media.

Within this multi-class room a medium-size group of students may be working together at the large central lecture—laboratory area, small groups of students may be gathered together in a project or seminar room, two or three students may be working together in the project areas, or individual students may be at work in a project room or at a lecture-laboratory station. The preparation room is located to supply and service the entire suite, while access and circulation within the suite allows the various functions to take place without interference.

Various types of projected media are available to the medium-size group working at their lecture-lab stations, as well as to the small group meeting in the seminar room. In the project rooms and independent study stations, television receivers, portable film and slide projectors, and the overhead projector introduce media as necessary in the learning situations.

In this type of multi-discipline, multi-class laboratory it is the use of media to extend the role and range of the teacher that permits such a setting to be justified and suitable for education.

PLAN   scale: 1/16" = 1'-0"

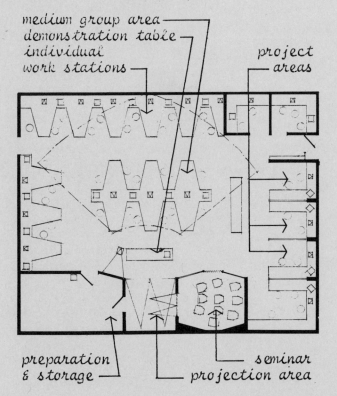

medium group area
demonstration table
individual
work stations

project areas

preparation & storage

seminar
projection area

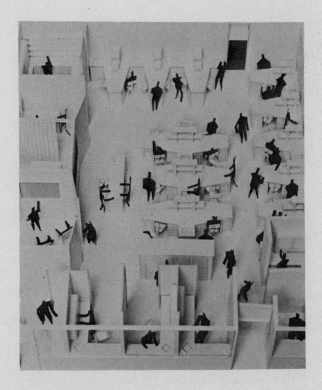

LG LARGE-GROUP FACILITIES

It seems that the effectiveness of media in education has been tested most extensively in large-group learning situations. Certainly in the last ten years many public schools and a large number of colleges and universities have adopted large-group instruction using media for an increasingly large proprotion of the instructional load. In fact, it is through the utilization of learning media that large-group instruction may become truly effective—by bringing to this type of learning system means for magnifying and displaying information, presenting information from a remote location, introducing information that otherwise would be impossible, and introducing information in a more demonstratively effective way.

There is a current re-examination of large-group instruction following on the heels of a general concern for more independent and individualized learning experiences. Even though there are proponents of each to the exclusion of the other, the logical solution for most institutions will be the incorporation of both types of learning experience—and indeed a variety of learning experiences in-between—and in turn the necessary facilities for their effective use. This "mix" of learning experiences is the basis for many organizational patterns, and is at the heart of the systems approach to designing learning.

For these reasons an examination of the planning of large-group facilities with media is essential, particularly because the design criteria and planning considerations in large-group facilities with media are probably the most critical of any type of space that might be provided. The following points summarize these design and planning criteria:

1. An optimum viewing area, as defined by the various display surfaces which are considered critical for student viewing, will determine the most effective room shape. This optimum area is not a fixed function of the combination of screens and/or monitors, but will vary with the type of material presented, the duration of the presentation, the quality of the equipment, the type of screen, and other factors of environment. (See Report C, for details of projection systems and viewing areas).

2. Stepped or sloped floors will always be required in order to provide optimum viewing conditions. Both horizontal and vertical sight lines in these rooms are major design factors. Also, raised seating introduces more intimacy in these rooms and may allow the interaction desired for case presentations and discussions.

3. Once the viewing area has been established, the actual capacity of the large-group space becomes a function of the seating type and arrangement. Seating types run the gamut from loose seats to fixed seats and built-in counters; Report C gives some attention to this wide range of available types. Whenever possible, aisles and circulation spaces should be kept out of the viewing area to assure the maximum number of seats located within optimum viewing conditions.

4. As long as the display of information and the use of media is a significant function in the large-group room, windows and natural light are a liability rather than an asset. Although means may be found for controlling natural light, the size of required images in the room mitigates against natural light with its inherent problems of control and "washed out images" caused by ambient light.

5. Complete climatic conditioning is necessary for this type of space by virtue of the number of students involved, the lack of natural windows and ventilation, and the concentration required by this type of learning experience. Such conditioning will include cooling, air change, filtration and humidity control.

6. Proper acoustical design, from the outset, is necessary for the successful functioning of this type of room. Not only should sound originating within the room be easily heard by all students, but the space should be thoroughly acoustically isolated from interfering sounds from the outside.

7. Likewise, the planning of lighting is an important consideration. Generally, three levels of illumination will be necessary for the display methods used in these spaces; control of ambient light on projection screens is likewise essential. Report C discusses these criteria in more detail.

8. Because lighting, acoustics, and climatic conditioning are such critical design features in the large-group room, their integration and design must be considered from the outset. Too often this kind of space suffers badly from neglecting these design features until too late in the planning process.

9. Educationally, the key to the proper functioning of this type of space is the integration of the systems for displaying information and other media uses. The studies which follow illustrate the fact that the display surfaces are an integral part of the room, and that equipment should be located for proper functioning and not to interfere in any way with the process of learning. This consideration includes the location and planning of the teacher's lectern or control center, and suggests that lighting and equipment be tied in and controlled from this lectern.

10. Finally, the success of these rooms will depend on the inclusion and relationship of adjunct storage, projection, and preparation areas. This is particularly true when rooms are to be used for science courses requiring equipment and demonstrations. In addition, these adjunct spaces may include project areas, conference rooms, and other smaller-group activities used to complement large-group presentation.

Large group instruction is sometimes criticized for being impersonal and lacking feedback and interaction between teacher and student. The use of student response systems can begin to put back into the instructional process an immediate indication of successful communication between teacher and student and can help make both instruction and learning more effective. The large group studies that follow would all be appropriate for such response systems.

LARGE-GROUP STUDY LG-1

This room is designed for 50 or more students with opportunities for displaying information which completely encircles the seating area. The 360-degree display surface consists of three media modules, TV monitors, overhead projection screens, and a large expanse of chalkboard and tackboard area. This concept of information display would be particularly appropriate in expository or developmental processes which are part of instructional techniques in science and mathematics; as the presentation or development of information takes place around the perimeter of the room, the students rotate in fixed, but pivoting, chair units.

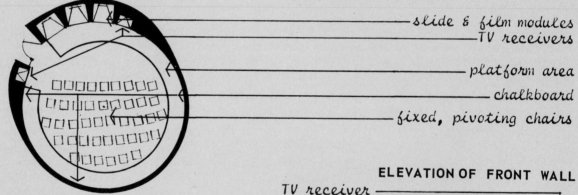

slide & film modules
TV receivers
platform area
chalkboard
fixed, pivoting chairs

PLAN

scale: 1/16" = 1'-0"

This kind of large-group room could exist by itself, or more likely, it would be surrounded by complementary discussion, seminar, and independent study areas. The most significant drawback is that the rotating seats will require a larger square-foot area per student than normal unidirectional seating.

The elevation of the front of the room shows the large variety of media potentially available for use in the room. The platform around the perimeter can be used by the instructor, and is important in providing adequate sight lines from the students seated on the flat floor.

ELEVATION OF FRONT WALL

TV receiver
audio recorder
media modules
overhead projection screens
equipment units

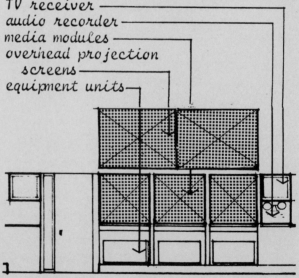

LARGE-GROUP STUDY LG-2

For a directional large-group room in which extensive uses of media are demanded, this study introduces some planning concepts. The plan and section indicate the variety of media modules and other display surfaces which are available within the room. All students in the space fall within an appropriate viewing area for all of these information display surfaces.

The seating is indicated as loose chairs located behind continuous counter tops. The horseshoe form of the seating begins to introduce interaction among the students as well as between students and instructor. In addition, the horseshoe arrangement permits a demonstration center at the front of the room. This form, too, requires relatively large square-foot areas per student.

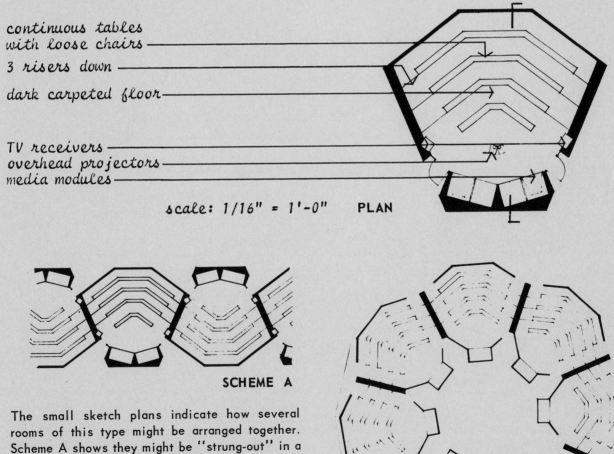

continuous tables
with loose chairs

3 risers down

dark carpeted floor

TV receivers
overhead projectors
media modules

scale: 1/16" = 1'-0"   PLAN

SCHEME A

The small sketch plans indicate how several rooms of this type might be arranged together. Scheme A shows they might be "strung-out" in a linear pattern and Scheme B indicates that they can be positioned in a circular shape around a central preparation area. In the latter scheme, this preparation area would be accessible from the front of each room, and would be particularly appropriate if used for science courses requiring this adjunct kind of space.

SCHEME B

LARGE-GROUP STUDY LG-3

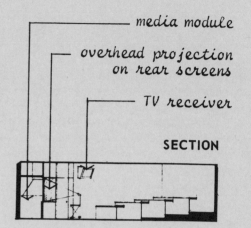

media module

overhead projection on rear screens

TV receiver

SECTION

Somewhat similar to the previous one, this study presents a room which may be expanded to house anywhere from 50 to several hundred students. This particular study illustrates a large-group room for approximately 60 students.

The arrangement of the display surfaces and equipment dictate a viewing area which in turn becomes the basic form of the room. The seating is arranged as loose seats behind continuous table tops and, like the previous study, there are no aisles in the viewing area. The small scheme shows how these kinds of spaces may be effectively clustered if several of them are needed.

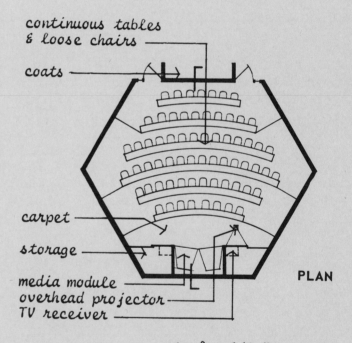

continuous tables & loose chairs

coats

carpet

storage

media module
overhead projector
TV receiver

PLAN

scale: 1/16" = 1'-0"

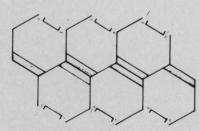

GROUP ARRANGEMENT

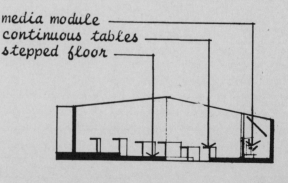

media module
continuous tables
stepped floor

SECTION

LARGE-GROUP STUDY LG-4

This study is for a group of 75 or more students, is basically rectangular in form, and indicates how two rooms of this type may be logically placed "back-to-back" resulting in better handling of projection and preparation areas for both.

The basic plan and model show projection surfaces in the front of each room, half of which are for rear projection, the other half for front projection or chalkboard. This combined front and rear projection scheme provides a wide variety of opportunities for introducing media into the large-group room.

The plan indicates loose seats behind continuous countertops in horseshoe form. Based on the viewing area defined by the projection surfaces, however, the actual kinds of seating may vary significantly. Countertops may be straight, seating may be loose, fixed, or riser-mounted on the stepped flooring. Even loose tablet-arm chairs may be provided on the platform steps.

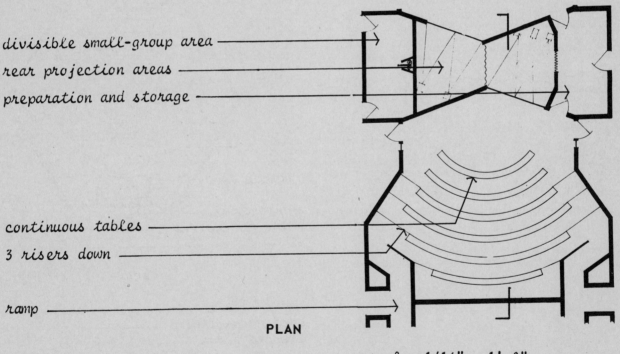

divisible small-group area

rear projection areas

preparation and storage

continuous tables

3 risers down

ramp

PLAN

scale: 1/16" = 1'-0"

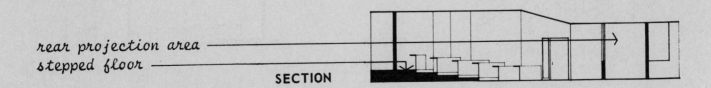

rear projection area

stepped floor

SECTION

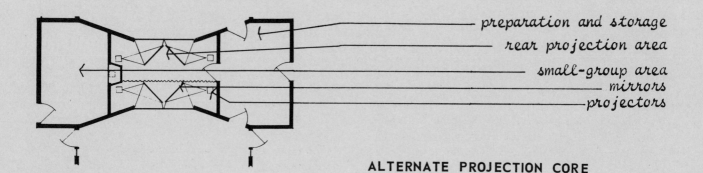

preparation and storage
rear projection area
small-group area
mirrors
projectors

ALTERNATE PROJECTION CORE

An important feature of this study is the service "core" which provides projection services to both rooms. Also in this core is a preparation and storage space, and a small seminar room for team projects, small-group meetings, or other complementary uses. The alternate core plan shows another way of handling these functions. The rear projection area is divided in half and, through the use of mirrors, projected images are available in both rooms. TV, too, can be rear-projected from this space.

The "non-rear-screen" areas in the front of the large-group rooms may be used for front projection, chalk and tackboard surfaces. Again common storage and seminar areas are provided for the use of both rooms. This alternate arrangement, with the projected images in the center of the front wall, lends itself to schemes where the room seating capacity may range upward of several hundred.

LARGE-GROUP STUDY LG-5

This study is really a combination of many of the schemes that have already been presented in this section; it indicates a suite of spaces with a large-group room seating 300 students at its center. Within the suite are provided a range of facilities from large to small group and from seminar to individual project rooms. Such a combination of spaces could logically form the core of a "school-within-a-school" or a discipline area in a secondary school. The storage, preparation, and projection spaces can also be considered as "support" or production spaces for media as utilized throughout the entire suite.

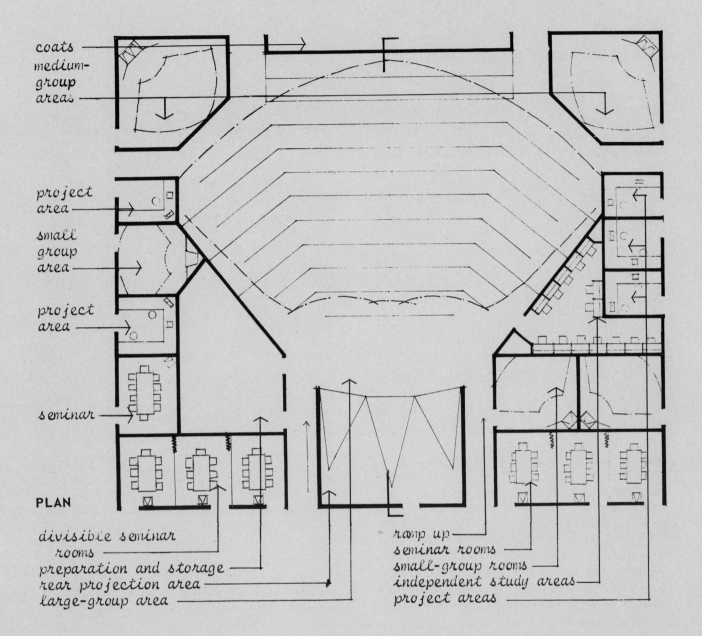

coats
medium-
group
areas

project
area

small
group
area

project
area

seminar

PLAN

divisible seminar
  rooms
preparation and storage
rear projection area
large-group area

ramp up
seminar rooms
small-group rooms
independent study areas
project areas

scale: 1/16" = 1'-0"

stepped floor in large-group area
rear projection area

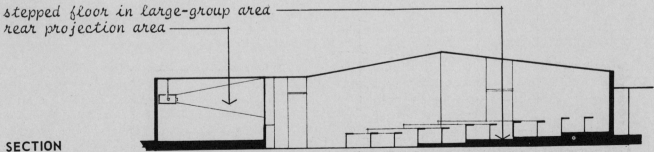

SECTION

LARGE-GROUP STUDY LG-6

Large-group instruction can include learning functions other than the simple presentation of information. Manipulative and laboratory types of experiences have been employed for many years, and this study suggests a combination of laboratory and lecture—demonstration functions within the same facility. The resulting "lecture-laboratory" permits the experimental and information presentation functions to be carried on simultaneously and without changing rooms. The advantages of being able to demonstrate and present information to a group of students seated at laboratory stations is one that may help overcome the problems of amalgamating media and instruction in science areas.

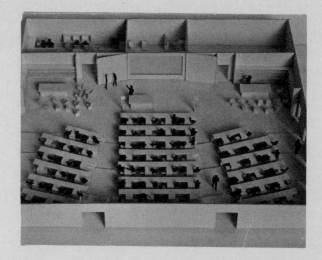

The lecture-laboratory is a suite of facilities including a large area containing over a hundred student laboratory-desk stations, two smaller demonstration and special equipment areas, a rear projection area, a special projects room, and storage and preparation space serving all parts of the facility. The student area is arranged on three platforms with a ramp at one side for wheeling in special equipment, reagents, and other materials for student use. Each laboratory station consists of a stand-up, sit-down work area with complete utilities serving every two students. The smaller demonstration areas in the front of the room permit small groups of students to work more intimately as a team or with an instructor, and also provides space for special equipment used by students during laboratory exercises; these can be shielded from the larger area by movable partitions.

The projection area allows two ten-foot images to be projected simultaneously, and further information display can be provided through two overhead projectors. The front of the room also provides area for demonstrations which are prepared and supplied from the adjacent work and storage room. These types of demonstrations will probably be magnified by closed-circuit TV and projected on the rear projection screen.

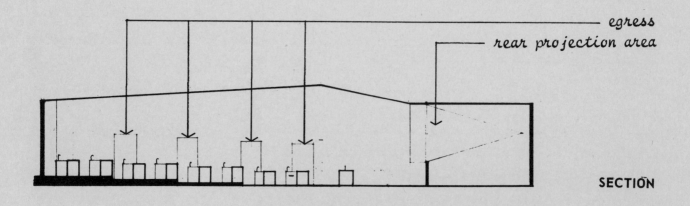

egress

rear projection area

SECTION

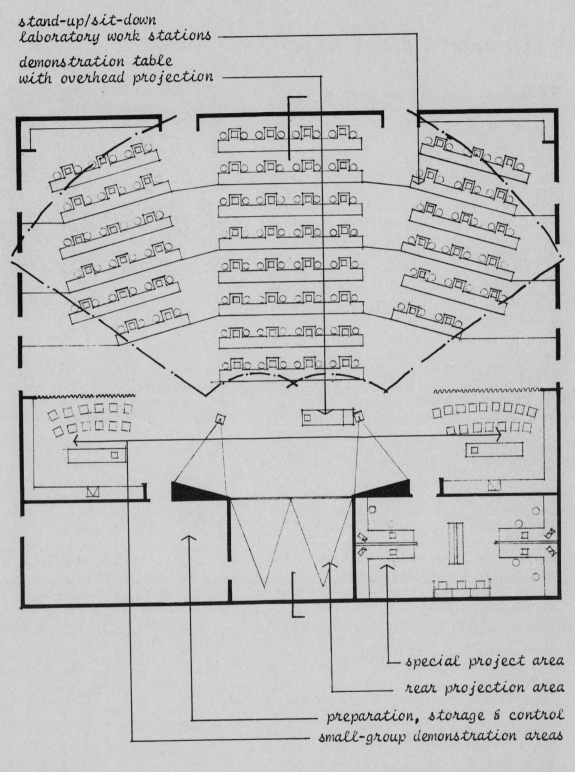

stand-up/sit-down
laboratory work stations

demonstration table
with overhead projection

special project area

rear projection area

preparation, storage & control

small-group demonstration areas

PLAN

scale: 1/16" = 1'-0"

LARGE-GROUP STUDY LG-7

In larger colleges and universities, large-group instruction may bring together 600 or more students in a single facility for instruction and presentation of information. Even in spaces of this size, appropriate facilities will permit the extensive and effective utilization of learning media.

This study simply illustrates some of the basic planning needs in designing such very large group spaces. The two floor plans indicate the upper and lower levels of a room seating 200 students in the balcony and upwards of 500 more on the lower level. This particular method of arranging students, and the logic of using the balcony, are borne out when optimum viewing areas are considered and sight lines drawn (see Section A–A). The most effective seating in this kind of facility would be fixed units with folding tablet-arms arranged in continental fashion (if local codes allow) with a central aisle and two aisles. Finally, it is obvious that in a room of this size and complexity, the considerations of lighting, acoustics, and climatic conditioning are of utmost significance.

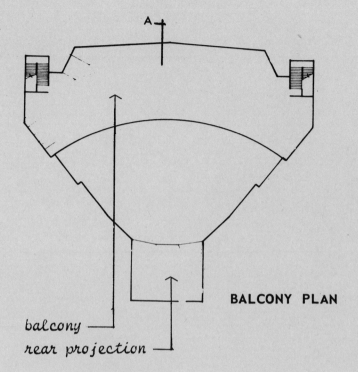

BALCONY PLAN

balcony

rear projection

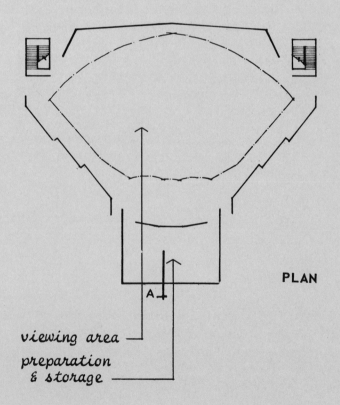

PLAN

viewing area

preparation & storage

SECTION A-A

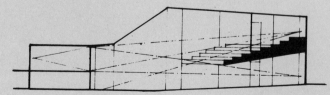

FG FLEXIBLE — GROUP FACILITIES

Certainly no single word has been bantered about as much in educational circles as flexibility. Flexibility has been seen by some as the means for accommodating future changes in contemporary buildings, while others feel that it only represents a lack of real decision on the educator's part. Some understand it and what it can do, others accept it blindly for what it might do and never use it. The significance of flexibility was discussed in more detail in Part 2.

Flexibility in spaces designed to accommodate media creates special considerations and problems of which the designer must be aware; there is always a need for optimum viewing conditions, and the problems of sound isolation in "flexible" spaces cannot be overlooked. It is, however, recognized that in some educational programs the ability to regroup students quickly, without necessarily moving them to another space, has merit. This series of studies has been developed to illustrate how spaces accommodating media can be designed to permit intermittent regrouping of students as learning situations demand.

There are some essential requirements to be fulfilled before these flexible groupings will work:

1. Money must be invested in high-quality movable partitions which have sound reduction capabilities of 40 decibels or more, which do not impose heavy loads on the structural system, which provide closure on all four sides, and which are readily operable by the teacher. While cost once prohibited extensive use of these partitions, further developments are sure to occur in this area, and the ability to rearrange students may become so significant in the educational program that investment in the appropriate kinds of partitions will be eminently worthwhile even before cost has been greatly lowered.

2. Regrouping students changes image viewing requirements. Creating self-contained media modules (see study SG-1), some of which are portable and can be moved as the students move, may be the key to using image-display media in these facilities. In the following studies, it will be noticed that, as the groups are rearranged, some of the media modules are rearranged; some are set aside and used only for larger groups, and others are positioned for use with the smaller groups.

3. It must be as easy to regroup the furniture as it is to regroup the students. There is a need for lightweight, easily movable, and preferably modular, table and chair units which can be used in all kinds of grouping.

4. Carpeting as an acoustical element is important to flexible grouping and movable furniture. The educational benefits derived from permissive regrouping can be easily negated by the sound and confusion of scraping desks and chairs over hard-surface floors.

5. A final point is directed at the need for special lighting and climatic controls to allow these rooms to work appropriately. The necessary controls—often elaborate—will certainly be additional expense. Specifically, lighting must be provided on a variety of circuits so that when a large-group space is divided into medium- or small-group areas the lighting can be controlled separately in each of the smaller spaces. Likewise heating and cooling must be zoned so it can work effectively in smaller rooms created from larger ones and vice versa.

Most of the flexible grouping studies which follow are most appropriate for elementary and secondary schools. Although there are applications of flexible groupings in colleges and universities, the traditions of class scheduling will generally allow the provision of a mix of spaces to accommodate the variations in group size rather than a series of flexible facilities.

FLEXIBLE-GROUP STUDY FG-1

This hexagonally-shaped unit could well provide for the flexible groupings desirable as part of a loft-plan school or as a focus in a "school-within-a-school." It could be surrounded with complementary independent study, project, conference, teacher work areas and resource facilities.

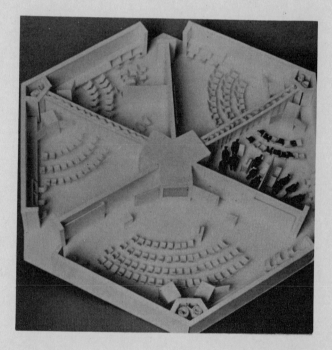

Each third of the scheme is a large-group space seating 60 to 75 students; the shape of these rooms provides ideal viewing conditions for the media module, the supplementary front projection surfaces, chalk and tackboard areas. By closing the movable partition in any of these rooms, and by folding in the "wings" of the large media module, two medium-group spaces seating about 30 can be formed. At this point, the smaller media modules come into use for the medium-group.

Any one of the medium-group rooms can be rearranged to provide for three or four smaller groups oriented to TV monitors, overhead projection, or the media module. The key to this further subdivision is a series of two or three folding panels which form privacy barriers within the medium-group space and which can be used for supplementary display or projection surfaces.

Finally, each segment of the scheme provides some built-in counter and storage facilities and three or more independent study carrels. These carrels may or may not be wired into a central resource area for audio and visual call-up of materials; they may be used for general independent study or may be allotted temporarily to students doing project work.

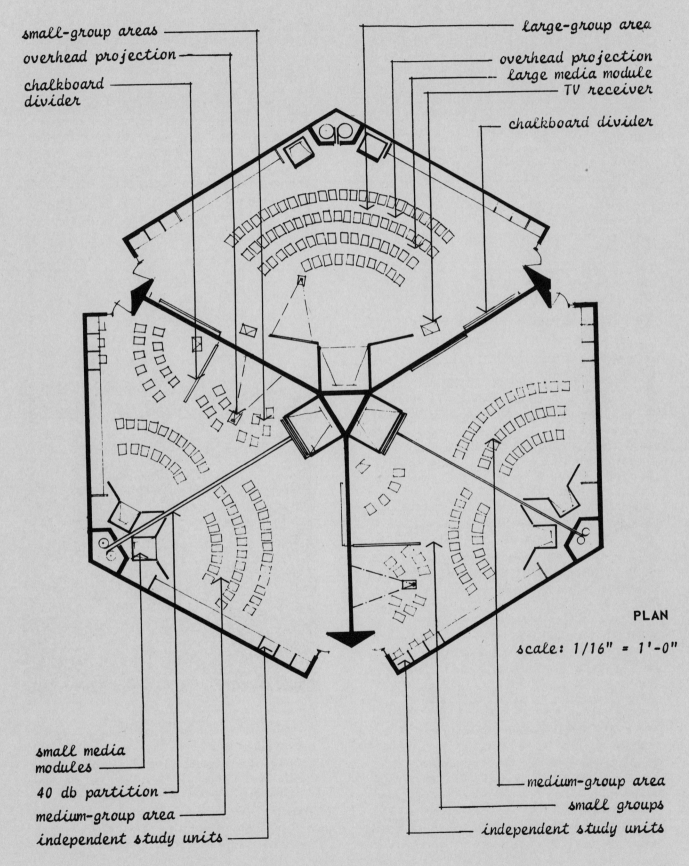

small-group areas

overhead projection

chalkboard divider

large-group area

overhead projection

large media module

TV receiver

chalkboard divider

PLAN

scale: 1/16" = 1'-0"

small media modules

40 db partition

medium-group area

independent study units

medium-group area

small groups

independent study units

FLEXIBLE-GROUP STUDY FG-2

This plan and model photograph illustrate another approach to arranging the elements of a flexible scheme. Here the spaces, based on a 60° equilateral triangle, are arranged in a linear scheme. The large-group space seating 60 or more students has the same provision for media as in the previous study; when the folding partition is closed to the face of the large media module, two medium-group spaces are created. These smaller spaces use smaller media modules located in the corners, and access to them is provided through doors located on either side of the enclosure for the folding partitions. As in the previous study, swing-out dividers can further subdivide the rooms for small-group activity.

large-group
TV receiver
media module
overhead projection

independent study units
medium-group
partition enclosure

chalkboard dividers
small groups

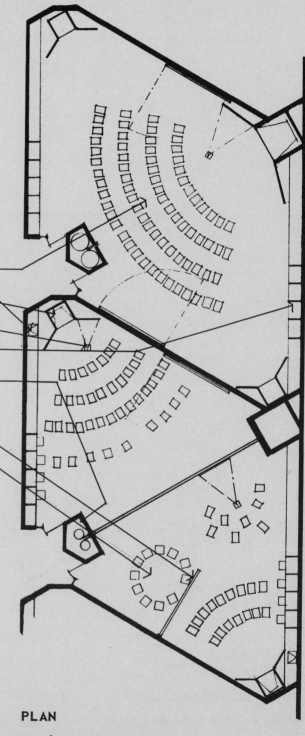

PLAN

scale: 1/16" = 1'-0"

By referring to the comments and drawings at
the beginning of the next series of studies —
Renovated Classrooms — it can be seen that
this scheme particularly lends itself to remodeling existing facilities. The linear flexible-group
rooms are 48 to 50 feet wide and can be incorporated in an existing classroom wing by moving
the corridor to the outside.

Within the viewing areas provided by this
scheme, as well as in the others, the seating
may be arranged to encourage interaction and
discussion through semi-circular and horseshoe-
shaped forms or it may be lined up for more
direct interaction between students and media-
instructor.

FLEXIBLE-GROUP STUDY FG-3

This scheme is based on a simple rectangle
combining six square modules of space. The
basic 30 x 30 foot module is designed for 30-
to-35 students oriented to a media module and
information display surface located in the corner
of the room. Within these spaces, the medium
group can be seated for interaction and discussion, for direct interaction with the presented
information, or for smaller-group uses.

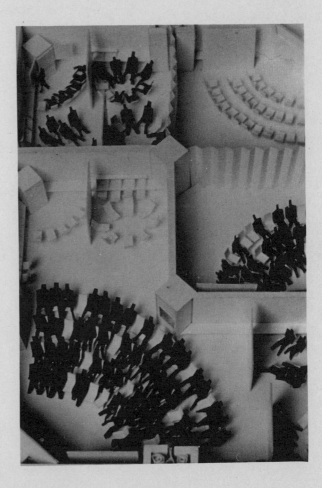

Three of these spaces can be opened together
and focused on a display surface with projection
originating from a self-contained projection cabinet located in the rear of the room; this becomes a front-projection solution. The audio
systems would be designed to serve each of the
basic modules independently or to be thrown together as a single system when the three rooms
are opened up as one. The projection equipment
for the large-group spaces is housed in a series
of self-contained acoustically-treated boxes
which are wheeled about and plugged in as
necessary.

It can be seen from the drawings and the comments above that this entire scheme is based on
movable and interchangeable equipment and display surfaces.

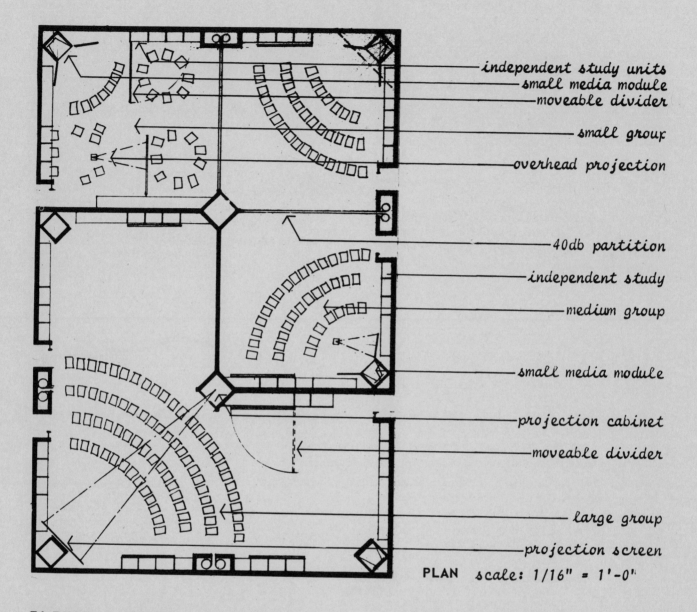

- independent study units
- small media module
- moveable divider
- small group
- overhead projection

- 40db partition
- independent study
- medium group

- small media module

- projection cabinet
- moveable divider

- large group
- projection screen

PLAN   scale: 1/16" = 1'-0"

FLEXIBLE-GROUP STUDY FG-4

In many schools and colleges the problem of economically utilizing large-group facilities, regardless of educational justification, is a very real one. For this reason, a number of attempts have been made to build a divisible large-group teaching space; the combination of smaller spaces with high utilization and the large-group room create a total unit which is more economically feasible. In general, however, there have not been many attempts to design divisible facilities which include media as an integral part of the instructional system. This study is developed to provide a large-group divisible space in which media can be used significantly.

The flat floor in the front of the room will seat approximately thirty students in loose chairs which can be rearranged for small-group, conference, or recitation presentations. The rear sections of the room are located on stepped floors, and seating may be on risers with continuous tables, loose chairs and continuous tables, or floor-mounted tablet-arm chairs. The dividing wall between these rear sections is a permanent one providing necessary acoustical privacy when the rooms are used independently. The folding partitions shown extend halfway across the auditorium and complete the division into three medium-group rooms.

Media are introduced into the rear sections through front projection of multiple images on a display surface located on the movable partition; the projection equipment would be housed in a projection center in the back of the room and would be remotely-controlled by the instructor.

When the entire space is used as a large-group facility, the large projected images are produced by a rear projection system. As can be seen in the diagram, two simultaneous rear-projected images can be produced if necessary.

The plan also indicates the manner in which these divisible units can be strung in a chain if several of them were desirable for a larger institution. The combination of flat and stepped floors, together with front and rear projection centers, render this divisible auditorium quite appropriate for instruction with media.

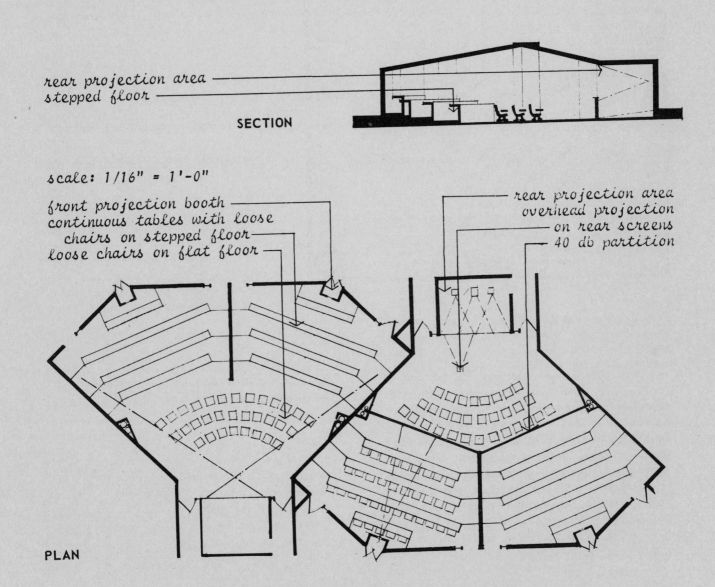

rear projection area
stepped floor

SECTION

scale: 1/16" = 1'-0"

front projection booth
continuous tables with loose
   chairs on stepped floor
loose chairs on flat floor

rear projection area
overhead projection
   on rear screens
40 db partition

PLAN

RC RENOVATED CLASSROOM FACILITIES

Probably the most effective way to introduce media into our educational system is through the renovation of existing classrooms. With over 120,000 schools and institutions throughout this country, there must be well over 2,000,000 such classrooms – a most significant "market." Remodeling but one or two percent of these rooms would go a long way im promoting effectiveness and efficiency in education.

These conventional classrooms—usually seating 25 to 35 students and ranging in floor area from 750 to 850 square feet – have long been considered the basic "building blocks" for school buildings. Not only are our existing schools full of these rooms, but they still comprise a great part of new buildings being designed and built today. From the standpoint of new thinking and new techniques, this may be unfortunate, but there are amazingly few administrators, boards, taxpayers or even state education departments who are willing to forsake the convenience or security of using the standard old classroom again and again. This serves to further increase the emphasis placed on accommodating media in the conventional classroom setting.

In this light, this section with its design studies and planning guidance is offered for three reasons: first, to give aid in creating a better learning environment in existing classrooms; secondly, to show ways of accomplishing this renovation; and thirdly, to suggest that remodeling can become a most potent force for introducing change in our schools and colleges.

By far the greatest percentage of existing classrooms in our schools are located in "egg-crate" fashion, flanking a corridor or circulation artery. This creates wings of classrooms 56 to 60 feet wide (two 24-foot classrooms plus an 8-foot corridor). The structural systems in these wings may run transverse to the direction of the corridor (as in Plan A-1) or longitudinally (Plan B-1). Despite the first impressions, there are many possibilities for remodeling within the restrictions of these wings and their structural systems.

If, for instance, the corridor walls in A-1 are removed (A-2) and the corridor relocated at the outside of the building, then larger elements of space are available for remodeling into large-group, seminar, and independent study areas. An arrangement of one such "mix" of spaces is shown in A-3. Plans B-2 and B-3 show some of the remodeling potential of classroom wings with the longitudinal structure; the only limitations here are the columns in the larger spaces in Plan B-3.

In addition to these general points, the following are are offered as more specific planning guidance in remodeling conventional classrooms to accommodate media,

1. Most conventional classrooms are rectangular in shape, often in a length-width ratio of 3-to-2, whereas the most effective shape for a media-oriented room is a square (see study MG-1). Therefore, one of the guiding principles is to select for renovation classrooms that are most nearly square in shape, and to design

classrooms with active teaching areas that are more square than rectangular.

2. Introducing media into the existing classroom may involve the development of some cabinet work to contain equipment and display surfaces. These "media modules" (described in study SG-1) may be built-in, semi-fixed, or completely portable, and may involve front or rear-projected images or both. Many variations on this media module are presented throughout the design studies.

3. Much of the renovation work in the school, including the building of the media modules, can be accomplished by carpenters, electricians and painters who are already part of the permanent staff of most schools and institutions. Rarely will elaborate and expensive contracting be necessary to make the changes.

4. Since nearly all classrooms are provided with some means of natural light, drapes, blinds, shutters or other devices will be required when media are used in the room. If media are rear-projected, the necessity for this control of natural light is much less critical that it is if they are front-projected. The exception to this rule is the use of overhead projection which, although it involves front-projected images, can be utilized in rooms with natural light.

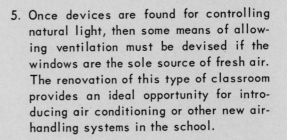

not in most cases!

5. Once devices are found for controlling natural light, then some means of allowing ventilation must be devised if the windows are the sole source of fresh air. The renovation of this type of classroom provides an ideal opportunity for introducing air conditioning or other new air-handling systems in the school.

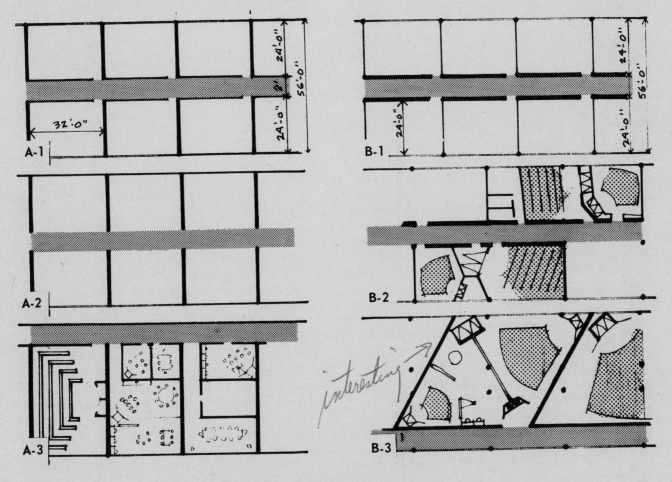

interesting

6. Generally, existing lighting systems will have to be rewired and recircuited during the renovation. This will allow for several levels of illumination in the room; these various levels are needed to compensate for variations in brightness among the media that will be used.

7. Flexible seating is necessary in a remodeled classroom. Seating needs to be arranged so that it can be focused on the various display surfaces, and the row-on-row, straight seating found in most conventional classrooms does not provide the best viewing area for media.

8. Remodeling classrooms should not be proportionately expensive. It does not usually require a complete gutting of the room. It does, however, require sensitive, creative architectural services in planning and design.

A final word on remodeling classrooms: they alone will not assure the use of media in the school. Consideration must be given for the

teachers using these spaces; they need equipment in good working order, a supply of necessary parts and technical assistance to back them up when necessary, and ready access to simple production services for making instructional aids. This should not be forgotten.

RENOVATED CLASSROOM STUDY RC-1

This study shows a conventional 24' x 32' classroom such as those found in many of our elementary and secondary school buildings. The outside long wall is a window-wall, and the room is served by one entrance from a corridor running along the opposite wall.

The remodeled Plan A shows the introduction of a media display center created through the addition of a cabinet occupying window space. This "window unit" contains projection equipment for the rear-screen projection and also includes chalkboard, tackboard and overhead projection surfaces. This media center, shown in more detail in the larger-scale drawings, becomes

the instructional focus for the room, and the loose tablet-arm chairs are oriented toward it for medium and small-group presentations.

The renovation of the room includes the development of cabinetwork on the inside wall and swinging panels to permit the room to be reorganized for small-group use as shown in alternate Plan B. When the dividers are swung away from the wall, they become tackboard, chalkboard, and overhead-projection surfaces. Depending on the scale of the furniture and the character of the room, either of these schemes could be used at practically any level of education.

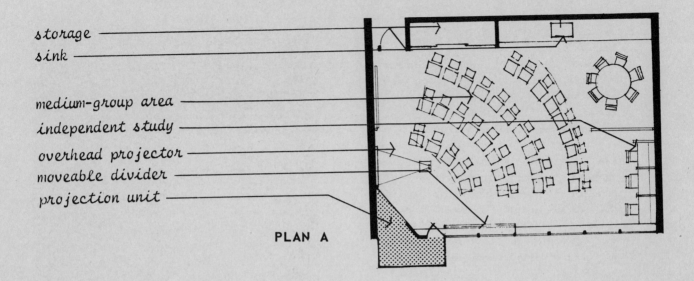

storage

sink

medium-group area

independent study

overhead projector

moveable divider

projection unit

PLAN A

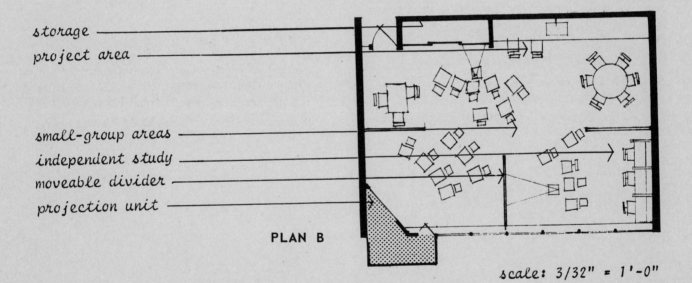

storage

project area

small-group areas

independent study

moveable divider

projection unit

PLAN B

scale: 3/32" = 1'-0"

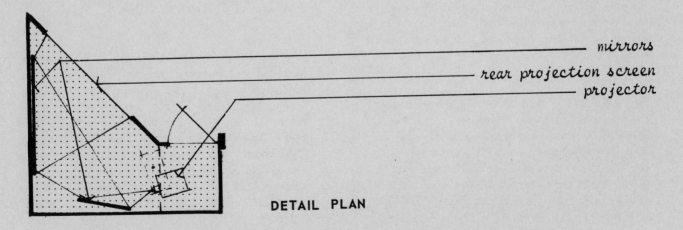

mirrors

rear projection screen

projector

DETAIL PLAN

RENOVATED CLASSROOM STUDY RC-2

The interior long wall of this classroom has been remodeled to include coat space, one or two media modules, television, audio equipment, sink and work space. The room may be used, as in Plan A, with the loose seating oriented to the media modules for medium-group instruction. Plan B shows the same room subdivided, through the use of swing-out dividers, for small-group, seminar, conference, project, and independent study uses. Here the dividers double as visual barriers and surfaces for chalkboards, tackboards, and projection surfaces. Small groups of students and independent workers might also find the small lightweight cartridge film projectors quite ideal for use in these kinds of situations.

This scheme has particular appropriateness for conventional classrooms where the window-wall has northern exposure, and the control of natural light is not critical. Of course, the use of blinds, drapes, or other control devices on the window-wall make the scheme even more extensive in its application.

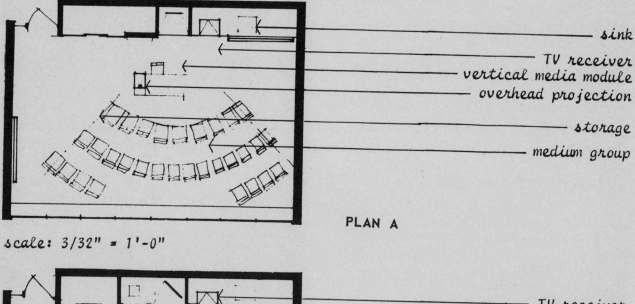

sink
TV receiver
vertical media module
overhead projection

storage
medium group

PLAN A

scale: 3/32" = 1'-0"

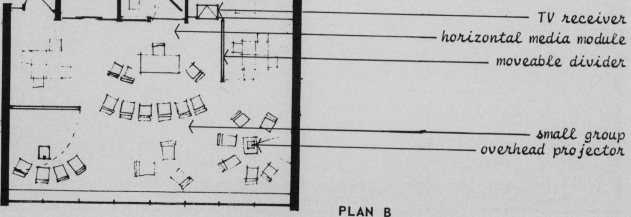

TV receiver
horizontal media module
moveable divider

small group
overhead projector

PLAN B

RENOVATED CLASSROOM STUDY RC-3

At the elementary level there are distinct advantages to the self-contained classroom, as long as within that space variations in grouping and activities are permitted. This study takes a typical elementary classroom and remodels it to provide these variations.

Plan A and the photograph of its model show the room as it would be set up for medium-group use with all students focusing on the teacher and the various display surfaces. The furniture consists of lightweight individual tables and chairs, and are oriented toward a media module consisting of a rear projection element and a screen for the overhead projector.

Plan B and the photograph of its model indicate how the same room can be subdivided for a number of functions including small groups working with films, slides and television, small groups working with the teacher, small groups working in ''dirty areas'' and on projects, and individuals working alone at study carrels. Throughout the school day, the students in a room of this type would move from group to group and functional area to functional area as abilities and progress demand; occasionally there would be teacher and media presentations for all to see.

This classroom could serve as the basic functional unit in a nongraded program as long as the program recognized the self-contained classroom in this role. It is also designed for multiage teaching, where there might be several groups in the room consisting of students at different ages but similar ability levels.

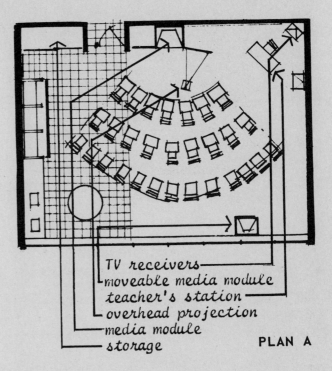

TV receivers
moveable media module
teacher's station
overhead projection
media module
storage

PLAN A

scale: 3/32" = 1'-0"

PLAN B

independent study units
overhead projection
moveable divider
sinks
moveable media module

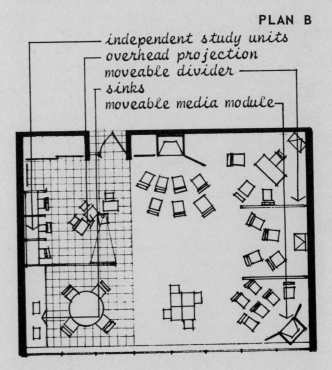

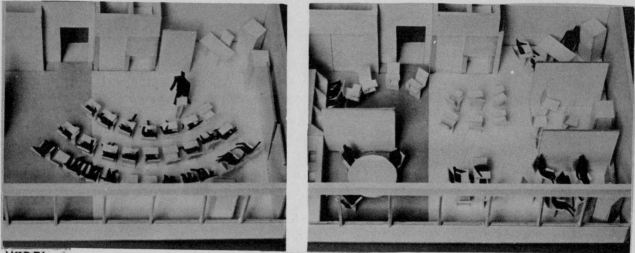

MODEL A   MODEL B

RENOVATED CLASSROOM STUDY RC-4

This study presents the simplest and least expensive method of remodeling an existing standard room. The media are introduced through a portable media module which may be used for 8mm, 16mm, or slide projection, and which contains a screen surface for overhead projector use. In addition, a mobile cabinet would contain a TV receiver and audio recording and playback equipment. Simple writing and projection surfaces, either attached to the wall or fastened to floor-to-ceiling "pole-cats," complete the installation. Light control on the window-wall is provided with drapes or blinds; this control must be quite positive behind the media to prevent glare.

The remainder of the room is not extensively renovated, but provision for rewiring and recircuiting lights would be necessary.

coats and storage
overhead projector
projection & writing surface
media module
TV receiver
drape

scale: 3/32" = 1'-0"   PLAN

RENOVATED CLASSROOM STUDY RC-5

Generally, conventional classrooms are arranged end-to-end along a central corridor. In remodeling such classrooms, some consideration should be given to the advantages gained from remodeling two of them at once, allowing more freedom in design and variation in spaces and functions.

This study indicates a basic classroom which may be placed end-to-end with other such rooms. Although some construction is necessary, this remains a simple and straightforward solution for introducing media in a series of rooms. The photo shows two rooms each set up for different functions. Two points are important. First, we see that by rearrangement of seating to focus on the display and TV surfaces, extra space is available in the room without compromising either comfort or capacity. Secondly, the use of the media center and other display surfaces permit, even in a simple classroom, a wide variation in media and groupings. In this study television can be used simultaneously with slides, movies, and the overhead projector; or any combination of these may be utilized if the program demands it. As in previous studies, the rooms may be rearranged for smaller-group activities. Finally, the rooms may act as a unit, allowing students to move from medium groups to small groups between the two rooms.

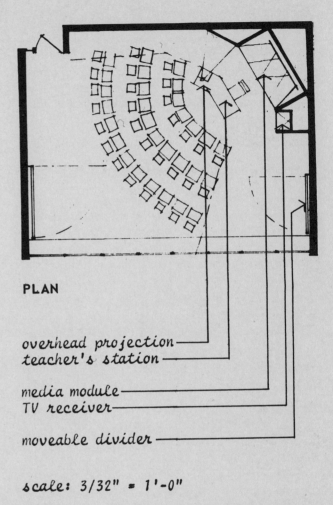

PLAN

overhead projection ———
teacher's station ———

media module ———
TV receiver ———

moveable divider ———

scale: 3/32" = 1'-0"

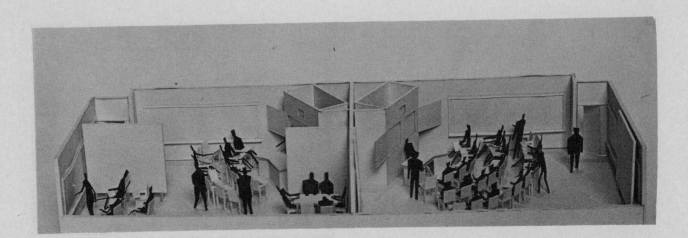

2 or 3 classrooms opened to make 1 room is of course the best remodeling.

RENOVATED CLASSROOM STUDY RC-6

Once two classrooms are considered together for renovation, a wide variety of opportunities opens up for the planner. This study, particularly appropriate for secondary schools and colleges utilizing large groups, reassigns extra space saved by seating rearrangements to large-group rooms seating 65 or more students.

The plan shows a third of a conventional two-room unit being used as a 30-seat room through the introduction of a media module and other display surfaces. Next to this has been created a rear-projection area, accesible from the corridor, used for displaying multiple images to the 65-seat room. This larger room has a flat floor

to accommodate the first three rows of seats, and then a four-step platform to provide adequate viewing from the rear of the room. The seating is diagonally oriented to focus on the major display surfaces, but yet to provide appropriate viewing of an overhead projected image and ckalk or tackboard surfaces. Riser-mounted seats would be used on the stepped platform, while the first three rows might utilize loose chairs and counters. This loose furniture, through re-arrangement, might allow the front of the room to function as seminar, conference, moot court, or case study space, introducing a new dimension in flexibility. In addition to the two rooms, there is a storage space for equipment and supplies.

PLAN   scale: 1/8" = 1'-0"

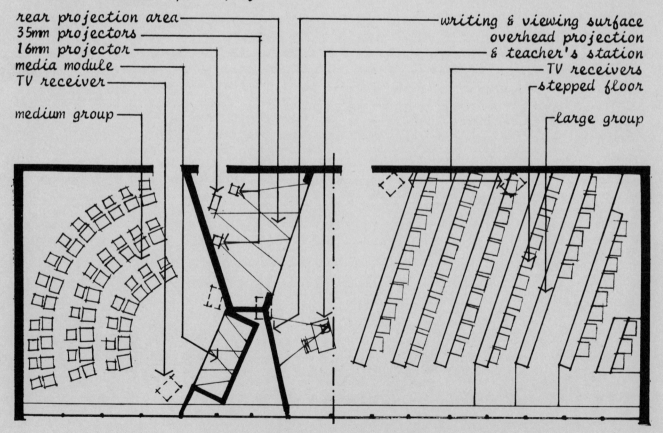

rear projection area
35mm projectors
16mm projector
media module
TV receiver

medium group

writing & viewing surface
overhead projection
& teacher's station
TV receivers
stepped floor

large group

RENOVATED CLASSROOM STUDY RC-7

Taking two classrooms together allows still greater refinements in facilities planning; they can be remodeled to provide suites of facilities supporting team teaching, variable groupings, multi-class teaching, or other variations now finding their way into schools and colleges.

In this study, several facility types result from renovating the two-classroom unit: a large-group room seating 50, a seminar space seating 20, a 6-man conference room, and two project areas. In all rooms, media become available for appropriate uses; in the seminar and project rooms, media are used primarily in the form of tele-

vision, cartridge projectors, and overhead projection. In the larger rooms, media modules for two simultaneous images plus television and normal chalk and tackboard areas are available.

Needless to say, this suite would require extensive rebuilding and re-equipping; it would be an expensive undertaking. It would cost practically as much to remodel this space as to build new school rooms. However, the provision of such a suite with its variation in functions and groupings and permitting extensive use of media, may be the most significant step any school or college can take within the context of its existing instructional space.

PLAN scale: 1/8" = 1'-0"

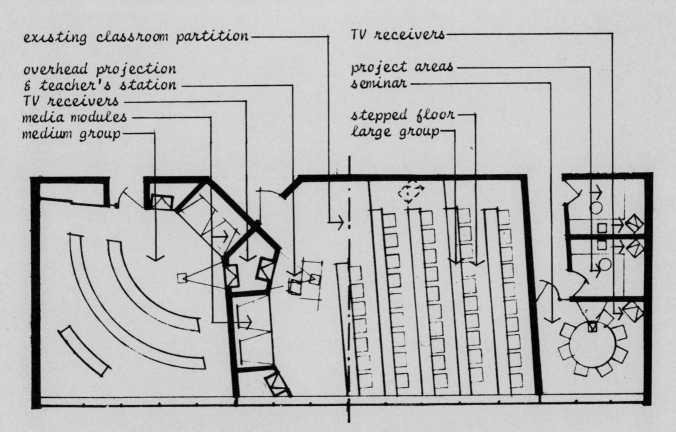

existing classroom partition

overhead projection
& teacher's station
TV receivers
media modules
medium group

TV receivers

project areas
seminar

stepped floor
large group

R F RESOURCE FACILITIES

No other educational facility is receiving more attention today than the library and its descendent, the resources center. There are many concepts and philosophies for the new form of the library, and as is appropriate in a time of change and innovation, the form of the library is certainly not set. One fact is certain; the library (it will be called the resources center from here on) is more than a repository for books and printed materials available for checkout or for use by students at long, drab tables with stiff chairs. The functional characteristics of the library are still present—the acquiring, cataloging, indexing, storing, retrieving, use, and restoring of information, but the information has taken on many new forms. It is in the form of books, periodicals, and standard references, but also films and slides, audio tapes and programs, video tapes and kinescopes, film strips and miniaturized equipment. The problem is how to handle these various types of resources logistically, and still have them readily available for student use as required by the educational philosophy of the institution.

It is certainly the educational philosophy and the way it is translated by faculty and staff that dictate how a resources center is used. It may be simply a more complex library—a place where students come and check out materials as required to complete assignments. It may also be the whole focus of the educational program for the institution—a place where a student comes and learns independently, and a place from which information is delivered to students throughout the entire school plant working in a number of different learning situations. More and more, the resources center is becoming the focal point, philosophically and physically, for many new school plants. Whatever the philosophy, it must be spelled out in terms of educational objectives before any architectural planning can begin.

A resources center may function as part of the system of education within a school plant in a number of different ways: Diagram A indicates a "little school" or "school-within-a-school" concept in which each subdivision contains a re-

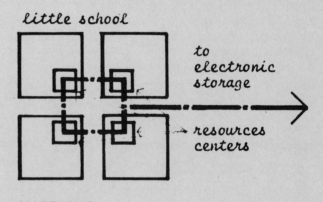

DIAGRAM A

sources center, either discipline-oriented or general in content. In such an institution, the resources center will contain independent study facilities and seminar and project rooms, as well as the resources themselves. These resources centers may be interconnected for call-up of material from any one of them, and in turn, all

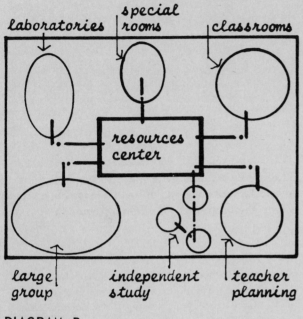

laboratories special rooms classrooms

resources center

large group independent study teacher planning

DIAGRAM B

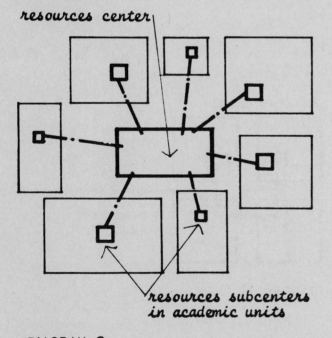

resources center

resources subcenters in academic units

DIAGRAM C

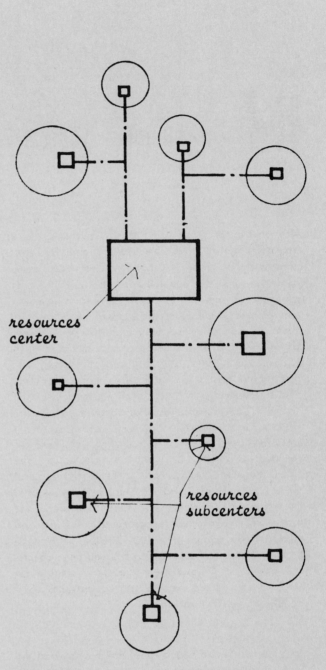

resources center

resources subcenters

DIAGRAM D

the resources centers may be connected with a large, regional electronic storage and retrieval facility.

Diagram B indicates a single resource center as the focus of the school and serving the entire school. Not only would students come to the resources center to use the resources, but audio and video materials would be distributed from the center to carrels and independent study facilities, classrooms, seminar rooms and other kinds of spaces throughout the school plant. In this case, a student does not have to come physically to the resources center to partake of its resources.

Diagram C might illustrate a large educational complex—a college or university, an educational park, or a large centralized school plant. A large central resources center serves the entire complex and, in turn, a number of subcenters located within specialized academic units. Here resources will be distributed in a number of ways and the student will have the choice of either using his local subcenter, or going to the larger centralized facility. In turn, the central unit could draw from large regional or national information centers.

In Diagram D, a central, electronically-based storage and retrieval facility serves a number of schools within a district, and each school contains a small resource subcenter. It should be noted that in this type of system all materials must be distributed electronically or physically from the central facility to the schools for student use.

In programming and planning resource facilities, the following points may prove of assistance:

1. The resources center in school buildings should be considered as a learning facility, as well as a place to store and and use materials. This means that the spaces must be readily accessible, inviting in character and environment, well equipped, humanely administered, and an integral part of the school plant.

2. Independent study and learning facilities within or associated with resources centers are more than "electronic carrels". A comfortable lounge chair, some carpeted flooring, a seat at a table, tables with low dividers, small separate rooms, and writing cubicles are all independent study facilities and should be represented along with the electronic carrel. There should not be a choice of only "wet" or "dry" carrels, but a mixture of these and other accommodations for individual students learning with resources.

3. A concern with space utilization has led to some solutions for independent study facilities in resources centers that consist of monotonous row upon monotonous row of carrels. Such planning seems to completely deny a basic philosophy of the resources center—individualization.

4. In bringing a resources center to physical reality, it may follow a variety of solutions—centralized in a single large space, decentralized in small units which are dispersed about, or a combination of both. Whatever the planning scheme, the resources center will include a number of common components. These would include administrative and work areas, media storage, book and periodical storage, soft reading area, independent study area, simple production and reproduction facilities, and conference, project and seminar facilities.

5. In planning a resources center, consideration should be given to the rapid advances that have been made in computer-based library operations — processing acquisitions, printing out bibliographies and special lists, handling check-outs and due and reserve notices, and requisitioning materials. Certainly this type of system should be studied with the idea of initially incorporating compatible components allowing expansion of the basic system serving several centers and subcenters.

6. Electronically based information storage and retrieval systems will certainly be a planning factor in designing resources centers. Some carrels will be "wired into" such systems for instant access to information, and in some cases, the resources centers may be part of the "input" into a retrieval system. The hardware and economies of such systems have not been clearly defined, and they are not universally available. However, planning must anticipate their eventual role.

RESOURCE FACILITY STUDY RF-1

This resources center combines many different types of facilities into a single center. As such, it would form the resources focus for a high school, middle school, and with modifications, an elementary school. In addition, it has many of the characteristics appropriate for a resource subcenter found at many points in a large educational complex.

The central area consists of storage facilities for books, media, independent audio visual equipment, and a variety of facilities for independent study and learning—soft reading areas, electronic carrels, reading and writing carrels, reading tables and chairs, etc. Surrounding this center are a number of significant supplementary facili-

ties. Small viewing rooms provide for independent and team work using projected media. Typing or audio rooms provide soundproof cubicles for individual use. Seminar rooms, project areas, and conference facilities all provide for the use of various kinds of resources by small groups working together. Naturally, storage, workrooms and office facilities must be provided, as well as reference files, indexes and a control center. Finally, the teachers planning, preview, and simple production facility is provided as part of this particular resources center.

This center would be located at the heart of a school plant with other educational facilities surrounding it, all easily accessible.

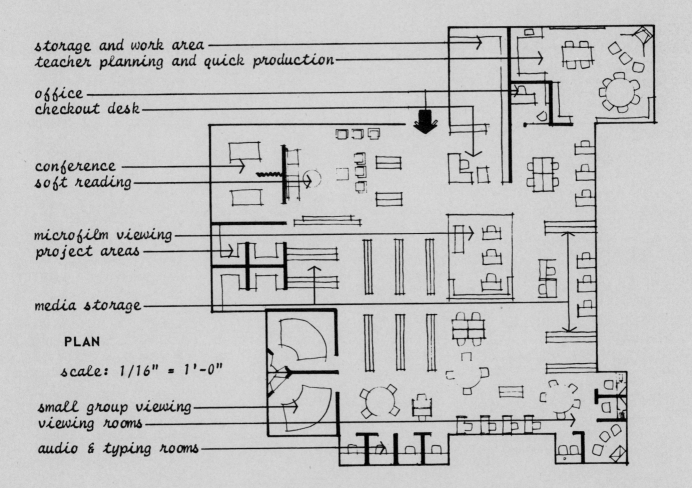

storage and work area
teacher planning and quick production

office
checkout desk

conference
soft reading

microfilm viewing
project areas

media storage

PLAN

scale: 1/16" = 1'-0"

small group viewing
viewing rooms
audio & typing rooms

RESOURCE FACILITY STUDY RF-2

This resources center would be appropriate as a subcenter in "schools-within-schools". It can be either a general resource subcenter, or discipline-oriented, and provides for long-term, independent student utilization. Carrels for audio and video use, and reading and writing, are provided, as are a soft reading area, tables and chairs, and enclosed and semi-enclosed rooms used for typing and recording. The adjunct facilities include small group viewing rooms, project rooms, conference rooms, a small teacher production facility,

and office work and storage space for the administrators of the center.

As a resources subcenter, this facility would be surrounded by other types of learning spaces, and the line of demarcation between the resources and other educational facilities would be undistinguishable. In fact, if properly designed, students would move between these spaces freely without feeling that they are moving from one educational world to another.

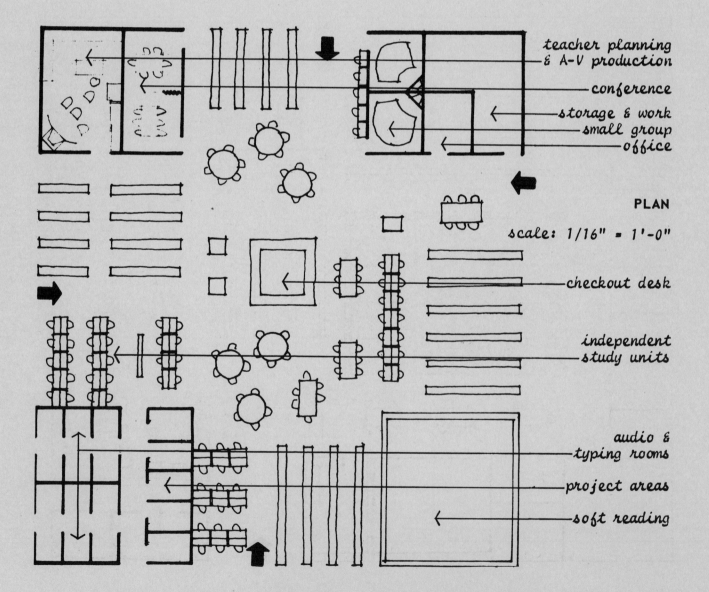

teacher planning & A-V production

conference

storage & work

small group

office

PLAN

scale: 1/16" = 1'-0"

checkout desk

independent study units

audio & typing rooms

project areas

soft reading

RESOURCE FACILITY STUDY RF-3

This resources center introduces the basic philosophic concept that teachers themselves are significant resources and coordinators in the use of resources. Therefore, they should be part of the resources center and this study includes a teacher planning and conference suite composed of teachers' work cubicles surrounding a common conference and work area. Here students may come on appointment, or on a "drop-in" basis, and consult with their instructors as readily as they could consult with the other resources contained in the center. This type of facility would be most appropriate for a nongraded or continuous progress-type of educational philosophy. It might serve either as a resource subcenter in a "school-within-a-school" concept or as the basic resources center in a school which is moving towards continuous progress, but which is initially designed for a significant program in team planning and teaching.

The remainder of the resources center includes accessibility to a variety of resources which may be used individually and in small groups.

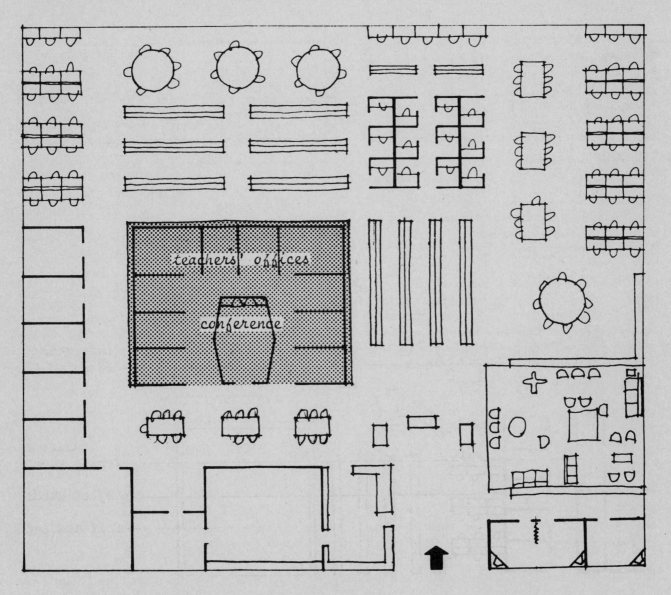

PS PRODUCTION – SUPPORT FACILITIES

To reiterate a basic point, the effective and efficient utilization of learning media in education requires three broad types of space—learning spaces, resource facilities, and production-instructional support facilities. In addition to classrooms, lecture rooms, laboratories, and seminar rooms designed and equipped with appropriate media, it is necessary that film, slide and tape materials and other media resources be made accessible to students and staff for individual use. Also, facilities must be provided in which learning media may be produced and which house the staff and functions that support the teaching faculty in their work.

The following points are offered as guidance in the design and planning of productional-instructional support facilities:

1. Production and support functions and in turn their facilities vary in complexity and size with their location and level within the educational system. Within an academic department or "little school" simple facilities should be available for teachers and students to produce transparencies, photo-copies, slides, multiple copies, graphs, and charts. Usually, this local, simple production area will be located within the resources center or instructional materials center; several were discussed in "Resource Facilities".

At the other end of the spectrum may be a very large and complex production facility as part of a large regional service and production center. Such facilities are discussed in "New Building Types" as they may form a part of the regional service center or educational laboratory. In between these two extremes are production centers which will serve a university, a college, a large high school, several schools within a district, an entire school district, or all the institutions located in an educational park.

The important objective is to provide several echelons of production and support ranging from the very large and complex covering a region to the very simple and local serving a few teachers. Also, to adequately support the uses of media, all of these echelons of production and support should eventually be represented so that the instructional staff has many levels to draw upon, depending on the complexity and needs of the particular learning situation.

2. Production support centers may be composed of a variety of components, each of which is related according to the echelon of production and the types of services to be offered. Some of these components are:

Graphic arts production
Photographic production
Motion picture production
Audio recording
Animation
Television origination
Television control, distribution, and recording
Film editing and processing
Graphic materials production and assembly
Scene, set, and model production
Equipment storage and repair
General storage

Administration and offices for production staff and visiting faculty and teachers
Conference and preview facilities
Film and tape materials and equipment storage and distribution.

In programming a instructional support center, it is the manner in which these components are arranged and placed together that creates the appropriate center for a particular institution.

3. The instructional support center can perform several major services in addition to producing films, slides, tapes, and other instructional materials:

- It can design and produce materials that are not commercially available, but which are needed for specific instructional purposes.

- It can provide technical assistance to teachers and professors in using instructional technology effectively. It is this type of assistance which helps teachers overcome a fear of mechanical devices about which they have little knowledge and great anxiety.

- They can be the catalyst which causes teachers to begin planning instruction and learning together. Producing televised instruction may bring cooperation among teachers who otherwise would always function as independent entities.

- A instructional support center can provide pedagogical assistance to teachers in designing learning. The learning systems designers—the pedagogical consultants—would logically be housed within this center.

- These facilities can provide the professional focus for teachers and faculty members by making available professional references, material, journals and consultants.

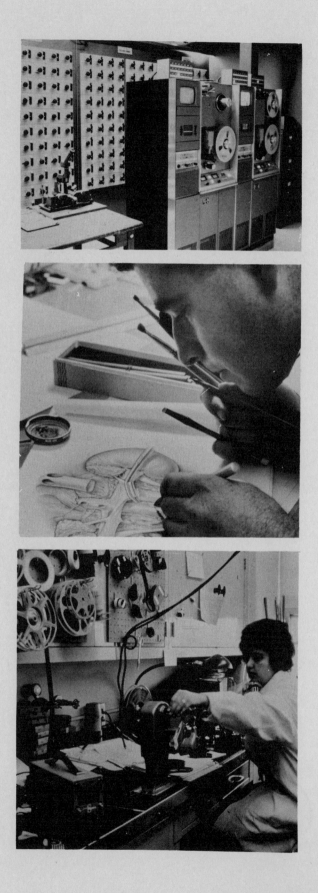

4. Instructional support facilities may be an integral part of an educational plant, or may be a separate, free-standing building or unit. In either case, consideration should be given to designing the area to permit changes in areas, and relocation of walls, services, and cables. Flexibility of this type is very important, as the functions and needs of a center will change as programs, staff and faculty develop. A "loft-space", free of interior partitions and permitting economical changes may be the best type of space.

5. One of the changes anticipated above involves the planning of TV studios. Often when studios are initially planned, the faculty will wish to provide for a class of students to be present in the studio during production. However, as the faculty becomes more comfortable with television, the need for students in the studio is less significant. The building should be designed to permit this evolutionary change.

6. Obviously there is no single instructional support facility which solves all needs at all levels. There are many, many different systems of production and support which can be diagrammed. System A indicates a regional center which supports a number of subcenters within schools throughout the system. From the subcenter further production and support activities are provided to individual classrooms, resources center, independent study facilities, and special rooms. It should be noted that within the resources center there is the small, simplified production area for teacher use. The same diagram might illustrate the activities within a college or university campus where, from a central location, major production and support feeds out into schools and departments and then into individual facilities and areas.

System B illustrates a center within a large central school which not only supports that school, but feeds into other smaller schools throughout a school district. This might be the appropriate diagram to illustrate production—support facilities within a "educational park".

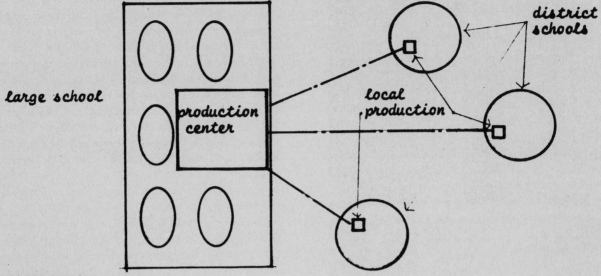

large school

production center

local production

district schools

DIAGRAM A

DIAGRAM B

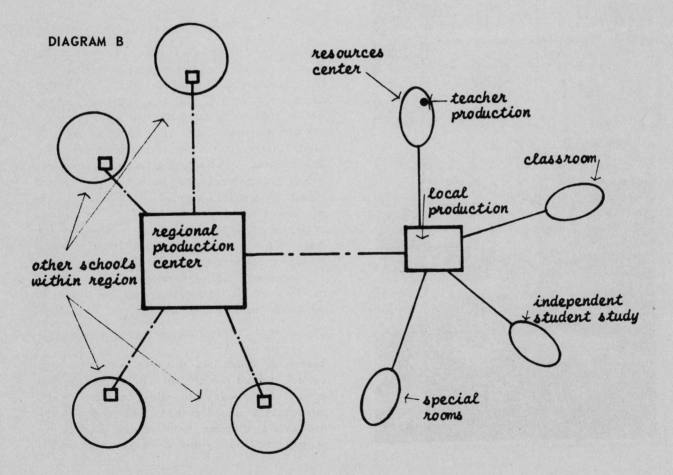

resources center

teacher production

classroom

local production

other schools within region

regional production center

independent student study

special rooms

PRODUCTION-SUPPORT STUDY PS-1

This production—support center might serve a high school, a couple of middle schools, several elementary schools, or a combination of all. Here are represented the basic facilities to support uses of television, graphic arts and projected media while providing the administrative and instructional support activities necessary for such a situation. The multi-use studio can be used for live and recorded television production, film production, still photography and, possibly audio recording. Control of all of these production activities would come from the central control and distribution room.

The graphics room includes drafting space, copying machines, film editing and copying equipment, assembly and work tables, and other equipment associated with these types of production. The preparation and storage area adjacent to the studio is used for building and storing sets and models; next to it is maintenance and repair area for AV equipment used both within this production facility and throughout the schools it serves. The administrative facilities includes waiting and exhibit areas, preview and conference rooms, and offices.

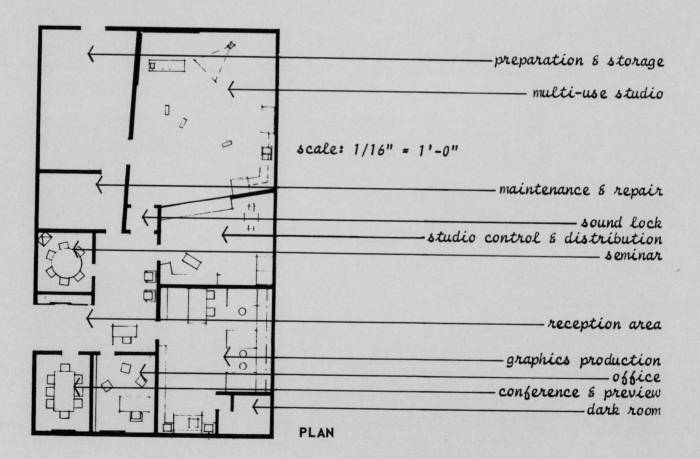

preparation & storage

multi-use studio

scale: 1/16" = 1'-0"

maintenance & repair

sound lock

studio control & distribution

seminar

reception area

graphics production

office

conference & preview

dark room

PLAN

PRODUCTION-SUPPORT STUDY PS-2

This is obviously a larger and more complex production and educational support unit, particularly because it has two multi-use studios which permit more extensive television and film production. This unit could serve a number of schools in a district, the schools within a educational park, a large central school complex, a college, or elements of a university campus.

The two multi-use studios both have direct access to the storage, preparation, and work shop area, which includes the service entrance facilities. The studios themselves are served by a common television control, distribution, and recording center in addition to individual studio control facilities. Other facilities include equipment maintenance and repair; graphic production with darkrooms, work and assembly, and drafting areas; and an administrative area with offices for staff and faculty, conference rooms, and teacher preparation and preview room.

PLAN

scale: 1/16" = 1'-0"

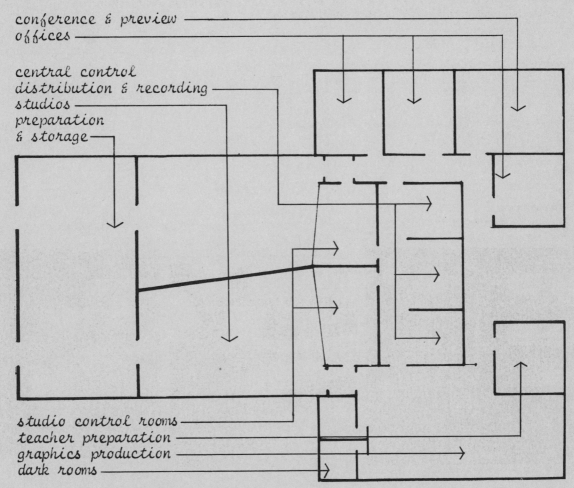

PRODUCTION-SUPPORT STUDY PS-3

This large production center is designed to serve a total university or college complex, a large school district, or may form the nucleus of a regional center. The entire plan focuses around a large, single, flexible film and TV studio with facilities located around its perimeter and feeding into the large central space. The studio can be set up in a variety of different ways and would have high ceilings permitting a wide variety of lighting arrangements and the flying of sets. Several productions could be going on within this large studio simultaneously.

Next to the studio is a separate control room and adjacent to that is central control and distribution, film and slide chain, and video tape recording areas. This would be the nerve center for an extensive and flexible TV system. Included in this area are audio studios for the recording of sound on tapes and films.

On the opposite side is a preparation and storage room with direct access to the studio and to an outside shipping and receiving area. Adjacent is a workshop producing materials for use in the studio and for direct classroom use throughout the institution. Technical processing, graphics, animation, editing, and film processing facilities make up a suite of rooms to one side of the studio, with staff offices on the opposite side. The remainder is composed of an administrative center with the director's office, conference and preview rooms, film, slide, equipment storage, and an adjacent maintenance area. The storage and maintenance areas would not only service equipment used within this production center but throughout the institution.

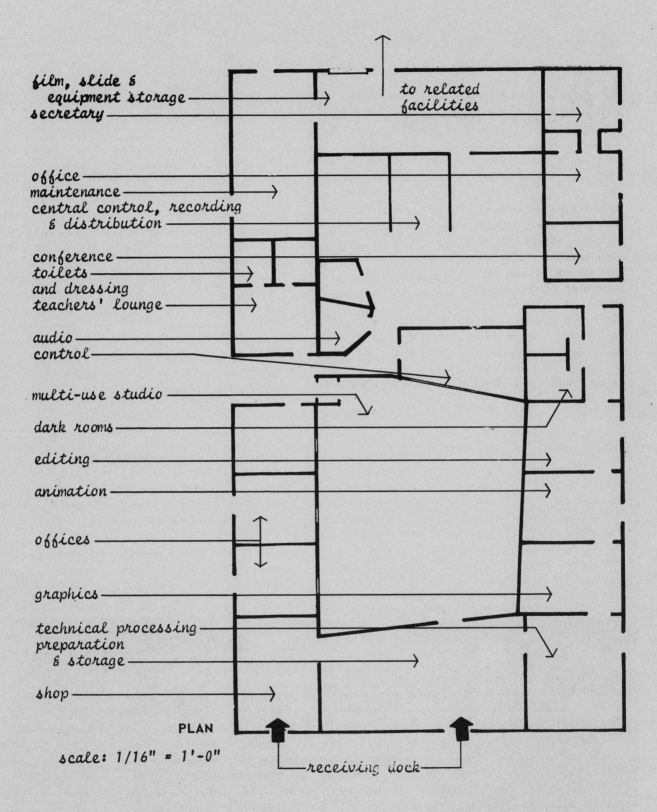

film, slide &
    equipment storage
secretary

to related
facilities

office
maintenance
central control, recording
    & distribution

conference
toilets
and dressing
teachers' lounge

audio
control

multi-use studio

dark rooms

editing

animation

offices

graphics

technical processing
preparation
    & storage

shop

PLAN

scale: 1/16" = 1'-0"

receiving dock

NB NEW BUILDING TYPES

So far these design studies have been concerned with investigating individual spaces or groups of spaces in educational buildings. This final group of comments moves into a different sphere. Modern educational theory and practice have suggested that we think of new ways of putting spaces (and other educational resources) together to serve new functions. Three of these new building types will be discussed in some detail: regional supplementary centers, regional education laboratories, and communications centers.

REGIONAL SUPPLEMENTARY CENTERS

Not unlike County

In these 1960s our schools are being called on to do more things, provide more programs, use more services than they have ever done before. Particularly in the field of instructional media is this true; the teaching situation is no longer just teacher and blackboard; he needs a great deal of instructional support to provide effective instruction. Students want more resources, and they want them faster. Media allows us to provide more kinds of instruction to more students, but we must be careful to provide the school with the "tools" to carry this through.

Educators are finding that this is easier said than done—particularly in regard to the economics of the situation. It boils down to the old paradox of excellence and economy—how can we achieve both at the same time.

One of the answers to this problem has been in regional development of instructional resources, services and programs. Schools and other institutions and community agencies are getting togeth-er to do things cooperatively that none could afford on its own. Title III of the Elementary and Secondary Education Act of 1965 has added impetus to this trend by providing support for these regional "supplementary" centers.

Participants in the supplementary centers are not limited to public schools. In fact Title III insists that other "educational and community resources" be a part of the concept. This includes public and private schools of all types, hospitals, libraries, churches, TV stations, historical societies, industry, professional societies and a long list of others.

The supplementary center can undertake a wide variety of programs and services for its members —probably no center will accomplish all those in the accompanying chart, but they are all possibilities. As one of the most vital concerns in education today, the production and development of media and learning resources will, however, be an important part of many of these supplementary centers.

In contrast to the regional education laboratories which will be next discussed, the regional supplementary centers will serve areas which are quite small—perhaps a dozen small districts (or two or three larger ones), or perhaps a small geographical area centered around a university. The advantages of these smaller-scale units are many,

- The supplementary center remains close to its members; teachers and administrators (maybe even students) can use it as a "second home" in which to research, to consult, to experiment, to observe, and to create.

- Since the center is a co-operative product of local institutions, each staff member, administrator, and taxpayer has a vital interest in it.

- Districts, institutions and other participants can benefit from working together on common problems.

- The center can serve as an educational "focus" for professionals in the region.

- The center can effectively disseminate research findings from other sources, and keep all participants informed on what each other is doing.

- **PROGRAMS . .**

administration, co-ordination, staff and facilities for special programs of all kinds: gifted children, college-bound, mentally and emotionally handicapped, culturally-deprived, disabled, technical and vocational, retraining, etc.

- **RESEARCH . .**

co-ordination of regional research and evaluation programs in many fields, including dissemination of research done elsewhere.

- **RESOURCE SERVICES . .**

central acquisition, processing and collection of resources; teacher examination area; search and bibliographic services; union catalogs of materials available in the region.

- **PRODUCTION SERVICES . .**

demonstration, testing and evaluation of media; origination of radio and TV programming; film processing and photographic work; making of graphics and aids, publications, curriculum guides.

- **CURRICULUM SERVICES . .**

small curriculum development projects; outside consultants and interim staff; professional resource collections for teacher use; adjunct and consulting staff in curricular and non-curricular areas; demonstration of new materials and techniques; in-service training.

- **ADMINISTRATIVE SERVICES . .**

aid and consulting to administrators in finance, law, transportation, etc.; regional data processing center.

There is an even greater advantage to the center —it has the potential of providing a truly integrated effort. The following example shows the real value of the center in developing and implementing a hypothetical curriculum change.

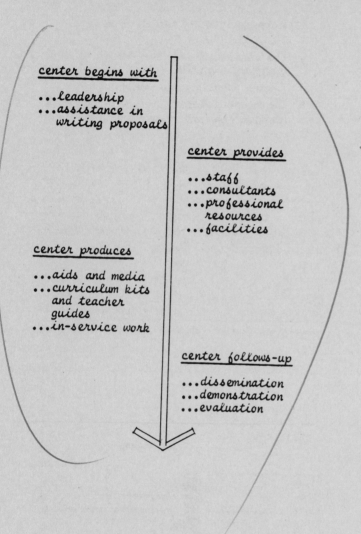

center begins with

...leadership
...assistance in
  writing proposals

center provides

...staff
...consultants
...professional
  resources
...facilities

center produces

...aids and media
...curriculum kits
  and teacher
  guides
...in-service work

center follows-up

...dissemination
...demonstration
...evaluation

This concept is not new. There are already many attempts to provide regional programs, resources, and services; some are little more than country film libraries while others (like Toronto's Education Centre) provide a whole variety of services, classes, materials, and publications. Title III money will begin to fill in the gaps in our fragmented efforts so far, and the future points toward more "comprehensive" supplementary centers.

Despite the constant use of the term "center," these regional activities may not be accomplished in a central facility at all. The best possibilities for co-ordination and cross-fertilization exist in the central facility, but economics may preclude this. Many of the programs and services can be accomplished in outlying or adjacent buildings; most "centers" will probably be a combination of a central building with many of these scattered adjunct buildings housing various parts of the effort.

The types of spaces that might be included in the supplementary center are many,

● Regional Administration

Administrative office and conference areas
Clerical staff areas
Regional research and conference areas
Central records and storage areas
Data Processing Center

● Program Co-ordination

Administrative and staff areas
Facilities for the programs themselves

● Resource Services

Regional office and conference
Professional resource library
Search and bibliographic work area
Central examination area for books, resources and equipment
Central ordering and processing
Central collection of materials for area borrowing
Necessary work areas
Shipping and receiving

● Production Services

Regional office and conference
Research, testing and evaluation
Equipment mock-up and repair
Radio origination studios and support

TV origination and support
Film origination and support
Photographic and film processing
Graphics center
Writing and editing publications areas
Publications mock-up areas
Central reproduction facility
Shipping and receiving

● Curriculum Services

Regional office and conference
Curriculum development and project
 center
Resource rooms for the various disciplines
Spaces for adjunct and consulting staffs
Student testing area
Pupil personnel services staff area
In-service training areas
 Demonstration classrooms
Exhibit areas

● Administrative Services

Legal advisory office
Financial planning, audit and control office

Transportation, maintenance, etc. offices
Central personnel interviewing and records
 center

● Supporting Services

Lobby and central exhibition spaces
Large-group area
Conference and assembly areas
Cafeteria and kitchen
Central receiving and storage
Central workshop
Maintenance, toilet, services, etc.

Many of these facility types have already been discussed in other sections of this Part 3. The design of the regional center will necessarily become a process of "putting them together" with the necessary offices, conference areas, circulation, and other "support" areas.

The following diagrams show the kinds of space relationships that might exist in a regional center undertaking a broad range of programs and services.

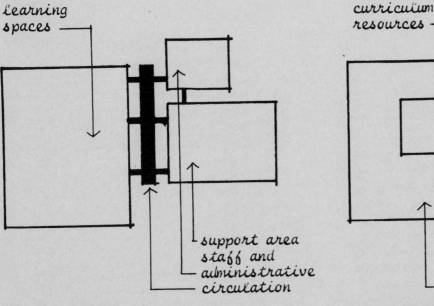

Learning spaces

support area staff and administrative circulation

PROGRAM-ORIENTED

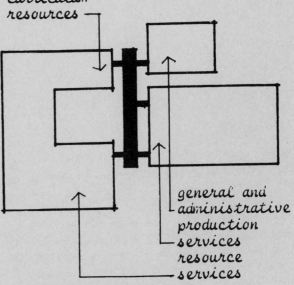

curriculum resources

general and administrative production services resource services

SERVICE-ORIENTED

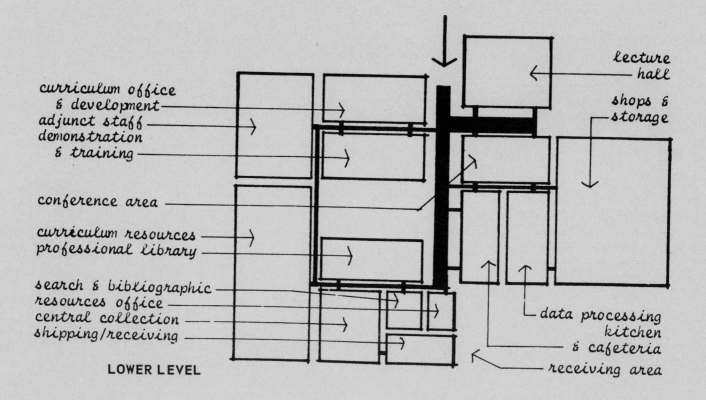

curriculum office & development
adjunct staff
demonstration & training

conference area

curriculum resources
professional library

search & bibliographic
resources office
central collection
shipping/receiving

LOWER LEVEL

lecture hall

shops & storage

data processing
kitchen & cafeteria
receiving area

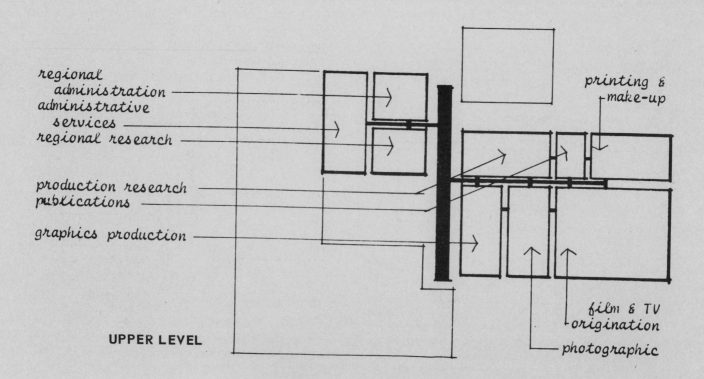

regional administration
administrative services
regional research

production research
publications

graphics production

UPPER LEVEL

printing & make-up

film & TV origination
photographic

REGIONAL EDUCATION LABORATORIES

Not unlike State

While the regional supplementary center can perform services and conduct localized research for its members, there is still a need for educational research on the larger scale. This larger-scale research has been growing steadily in this post-Sputnik era, but much remains to be done. Moreover, overall co-ordination of projects and widespread reporting of findings is needed if the research is to become an effective part of contemporary education.

These concerns stand behind the creation of the regional education laboratory. The laboratory steps in to undertake the research and fill the gaps always present between projects and dissemination of results.

So far, attempts at these regional research and development centers have been sporadic; some highly successful ones have been set up in large universities to attack specific educational problems, but the educational laboratory concept has yet to be adopted on any scale. Title IV of the Elementary and Secondary Education Act of 1965 calls for aid to support and maintain these kinds of centers, though, and growth in this direction is bound to result.

While these laboratories will take on different tasks, they will have some similar goals in mind,

- To carry on a concentrated and co-ordinated program of educational research activities. These activities will most likely be accomplished by eminently qualified persons, and will have widespread rather than limited application and use.

- To develop new curriculum units, with special attention to ways of supporting them. This will make media research, testing, and evaluation an important part of the laboratory's program.

- To test, evaluate and disseminate innovations on a broad scale.

- To provide direction and to encourage innovation in other quarters.

- To supplement and co-ordinate research throughout the region.

- To provide a training ground for educational research personnel.

In order to achieve these goals, the various regional education laboratories will have a number of common characteristics,

- Projects may be undertaken "in-house" or in collaboration with other educational and community groups.

- Staffing will include at least a corps of administrators to co-ordinate activities, a professional evaluation staff, and a professional dissemination unit. Actual project research may be carried on by other staff members, interim staff, consultants, or a combination of these.

- The laboratory will remain flexible. It will adapt to the situation as necessary, changing its own character as it undertakes different kinds of projects in different fields.

The regions covered by these laboratories will be necessarily large; some now envision perhaps a dozen large centers around the country. Smaller, more specialized units in colleges and universities may supplement the laboratories or extend their work into specific areas.

Implications for facilities, then, are not concrete. Most laboratories will require a variety of spaces, some of which may be "eeked out" of local college buildings or those of other co-operating groups. While many of the laboratory's activities may be scattered around the region it serves, it is reasonable to believe that there will be at least a central administrative facility and staff. Kinds of facilities may include,

- Administrative and Project

    Central administrative offices
    Conference areas
    Small project offices closely tied to central media and information complexes

- Central Information Complex

    Warehouse of resources, reports, data files, etc.
    May include Information Retrieval and Storage.
    Entire complex readily accessible to all in the center and wired to adjunct units of the laboratory

- Central Media Complex

    Production and origination facilities as required
    Work areas for testing and mocking-up media units

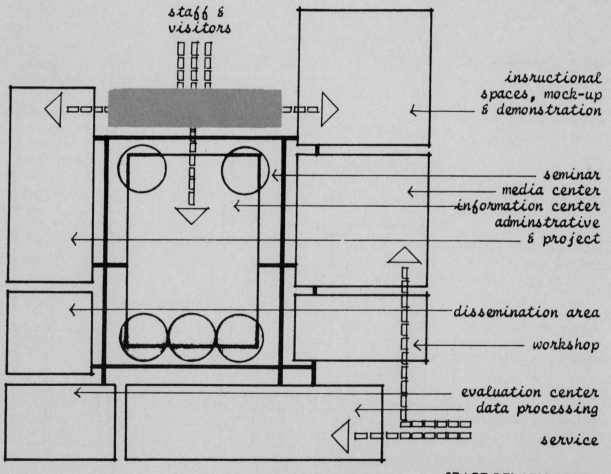

SPACE RELATIONSHIPS

Accessible to all functions in the laboratory
Can be used for media research and support for other research

● Evaluation and Processing

Office and conference area for the evaluation team
Data processing center serving all units of the laboratory

● Demonstration and Mock-up

Area for mocking-up different facility types
Large open space that can be arranged in many ways

Central location for access by staff, students, visitors
Provision for visitors and viewing

● Dissemination Area

Office area for professional dissemination staff
Publications editing and mock-up areas
Printing and finishing areas
Shipping and receiving

● Service and Workshop

Large workshop to serve for all "carpentry" activities in the laboratory
Conventional building service spaces

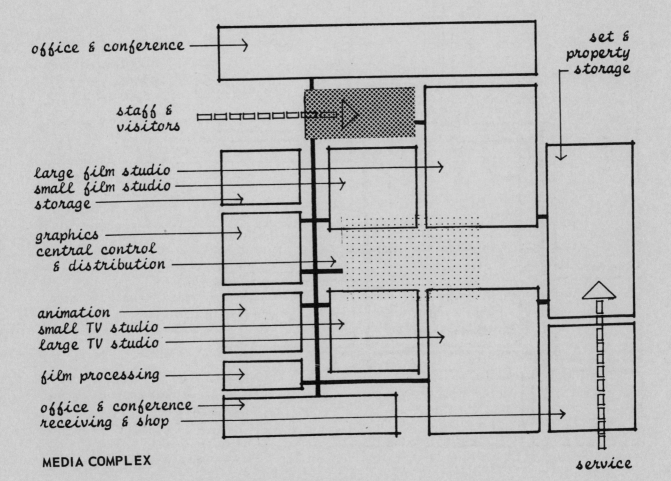

office & conference

set & property storage

staff & visitors

large film studio
small film studio
storage

graphics
central control
& distribution

animation
small TV studio
large TV studio

film processing

office & conference
receiving & shop

MEDIA COMPLEX

service

COMMUNICATIONS CENTERS

Basically production

Another building type resulting from new thinking and practice is the communications center. The emphasis of this type of facility is on large-group instruction and on the media to support it. For this reason, it is becoming a college building, centrally located on the campus to accommodate many hundreds of students in large-groups throughout the day. It may also be part of an educational park with its facilities available to all school groups in the area.

The philosophy behind the communications center is a simple one. If the institution feels that large-group instruction fits its needs for economical but effective instruction (as many colleges do believe), it makes sense to put these expensive "supporting" function together. The communications center can economically provide:

- Shared projection areas, allowing expensive equipment to be kept together in one room. This not only insures better care of the equipment, but through consolidation, utilization rates can go up.

- Special and expensive lighting and mechanical systems. It is cheaper and less cumbersome, for instance, to air-condition one whole building rather than little pieces of many buildings.

- Special and expensive electrical installations.

- Accommodation for weird room shapes; placing one pie-shaped lecture room in many separate buildings creates waste space and odd configurations. Putting many such rooms together in one building allows the good designer to cut down if not eliminate these wasted spaces.

- Centralization of production facilities. Since many of the items produced will be used in the large-group lectures, it makes

sense to consolidate all production and "support" activities in the building.

- A central "focal" point for faculty training in effectively using presentation and other instructional media.

The communications center does not become the property of any one discipline or department on campus; its use will be encouraged for all departments needing it. It will occupy a focal point on the campus, probably at the crossroads of major circulation paths.

The types of facilities the communications center may include cover those in many areas,

- Lobby and Circulation

    Include display, exhibition, reception, kitchen areas
    Generous to accommodate many large groups in the building

- Instructional Spaces

    Lecture halls (capacity determined by local programming)
    Storage and preparation areas
    Seminar and small-group rooms

- Film and TV Production

    TV and film studios
    Central engineering and control
    Dressing and ante areas
    Equipment storage and work rooms
    Prop storage and work rooms
    Staff and faculty offices
    Film processing and editing
    Preview and conference rooms

- Graphics and Aids Production

    Art and finishing studios
    Photo and finishing studios
    Staff and preview areas

- Instructional Materials Distribution

    Storage of materials and equipment
    Check-out area
    Office, records, and work area

- Administration and Research

    Office and conference
    Library
    Records storage

- General Services

    Workshop areas
    Shipping and Receiving
    Building maintenance

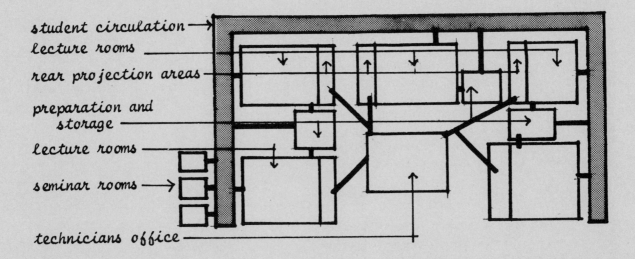

student circulation
lecture rooms
rear projection areas
preparation and storage
lecture rooms
seminar rooms
technicians office

SPACE RELATIONSHIPS

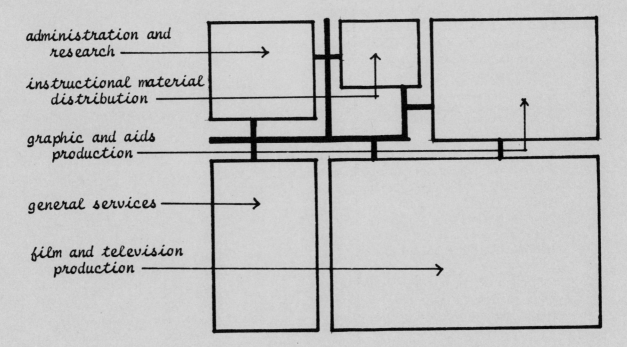

administration and research
instructional material distribution
graphic and aids production
general services
film and television production

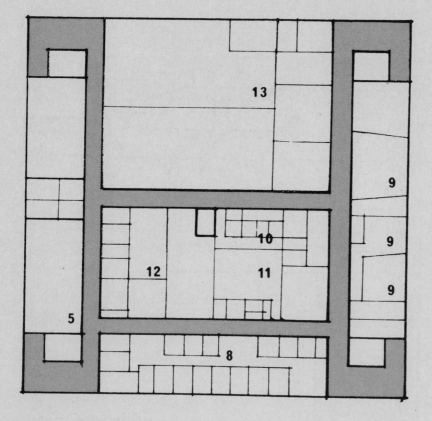

STATE UNIVERSITY
OF NEW YORK AT
OSWEGO, NEW YORK

communications
lecture hall center

Skidmore, Owings
& Merrill, Architects

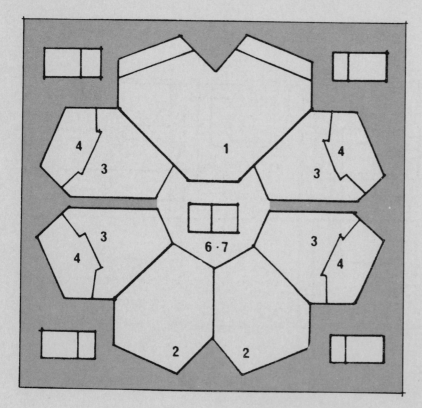

1 Lecture (480)
2 Lecture (240)
3 Lecture (120)
4 Lecture (60)
5 Assembly area

6 Rear projection
7 Preparation
    and storage

8 Office and
    conference
9 TV studios
10 Graphic arts
11 Photo area
12 Production
    storage

13 Mechanical
    and storage

STATE UNIVERSITY
OF NEW YORK AT
ONEONTA, NEW YORK

communications
lecture hall center

Toole & Angerame,
Architects

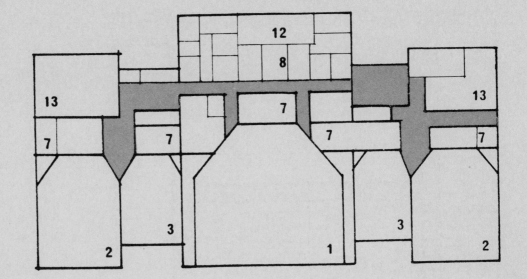

1 Lecture (480)
2 Lecture (240)
3 Lecture (120)
4 Lecture (60)
5 Assembly area

6 Rear projection
7 Preparation
 and storage

8 Office and
 conference
9 TV studios
10 Graphic arts
11 Photo area
12 Production
 storage

13 Mechanical
 and storage

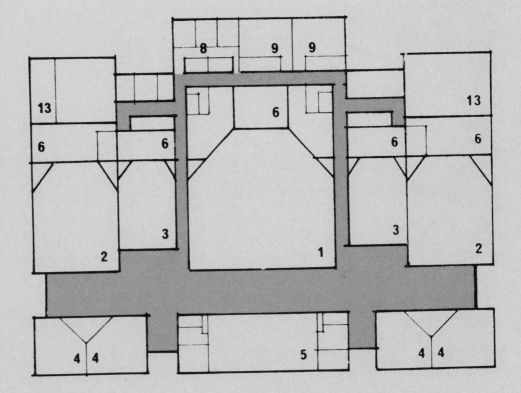

4 DESIGN CRITERIA: AN OVERVIEW

*This is a review
of Report C—
"A Technical Guide"*

A basic premise of this series of reports is that for effective and efficient utilization of media new concepts of facilities and their design must be developed. This Report B has presented general planning principles and design guidance for a variety of facilities developed for uses of media. It is also necessary to delve into the details of design—lighting, acoustics, climate, projection systems, equipment, furniture, and the like. Report C—"A Technical Guide" presents this type of information; here it is simply reviewed for those generally concerned with planning and design.

CREATING THE ENVIRONMENT

Lighting

Appropriate lighting is an important design feature that must be considered early in planning. Since the display of projected information is a major design factor in most spaces, two or three levels of illumination should be available in order to create lighting which is compatible with the wide variations in image brightness. Ambient light—stray light falling on screen surfaces—must be held within tolerable levels to avoid "washing-out" images. This is not as serious a problem in rear projection as it is with front projection; spaces which have natural light also pose special problems of controlling stray light. In all cases, regardless of the medium being used, enough light must be available to allow note-taking, reference to printed materials, and eye-to-eye contact. Within a learning space, all primary task surfaces should appear about equally bright, and the surrounding environment should be no less than 1/10 as bright. Bright trim or any sources of glare should be avoided. Control of lighting should consist of pre-determined levels activated by the teacher or by the projection equipment.

Acoustics

Good hearing conditions are essential in facilities with media even though uses of recorded sound cause conflicts with the trend toward open planning and flexibility. Acoustical design must control the passage of unwanted sound between spaces, the distribution of sound within a space, and the level of acceptable background noise. Basic laws of physics involving the nature of partition materials, the sound reflectance and absorptive qualities of surfaces and materials, the distribution of sound waves within a space, and the leakage or spill of sound between spaces must all be considered at the outset of design in order to create an acoustically satisfactory environment. Good acoustics begin with initial planning and end with the installation of proper amplification systems for recorded sound. In between are many important design decisions.

Climate

A proper learning environment includes a climate in which the student is alert and attentive. Usually this involves cooling the air (often more of a problem than heating), dehumidification, and ventilation. Mechanical systems must be designed to respond quickly to variations in heat output by students, equipment, and lighting, but which will maintain even temperatures and avoid drafts. The location of equipment to avoid disturbing noises and transmission of sounds between spaces is important.

FURNISHING THE ENVIRONMENT

Plan furniture
and casework
early

Too often the selection of furnishings for learning spaces is left undone until money, time, energy and professional assistance have been dissipated. Furniture should be considered as a part of the total facility, should be planned and selected early, and should meet basic aesthetic, functional and economic criteria. With so many types of furniture and casework needed to complete a school plant, and with so many products to choose from for each type, careful analysis and extensive research will be required for completely satisfactory results.

Three types
of seating...

In learning spaces with media, seating is of three basic types—fixed, moveable, and combined. Each has particular applications, and in some rooms a mixture of two or three types may best meet functional requirements. With projected media, fixed seating has the advantage of assuring that every occupant is in the proper relationship to display surfaces; many kinds of fixed seating are available—individual seats with various writing surfaces, continuous writing surfaces with various individual seats, and multiple units of writing surface and seat. The individual seats often have the disadvantage of inadequately sized tablet arms; the continuous writing surfaces solve this, but require more floor area per student.

*...each with
appropriate
applications*

Many, many kinds of moveable seating are available, some with combined writing surface and seat and some with these separate. Obtaining large writing surfaces is a problem; also, when seating is selected to allow flexible groupings, it is an advantage to employ modular writing surfaces which can form seminar tables or discussion groupings: Often a mix of several types of moveable seating will solve the variety of needs within a single space. Finally, a combination of fixed writing surface and loose seat will be an appropriate solution in some medium-sized rooms.

*Other kinds of
furnishings
complete the
environment*

Other kinds of furniture are necessary to complete learning spaces— storage units, teachers stations, lecterns, work counters with sinks and utilities, and cabinets with screens, projectors and other media equipment. The latter ''media modules'' have been discussed in detail in conjunction with the planning studies in Part 3 of this report. In all cases, this furniture and casework should be designed and selected as an integral part of the space; this should be a responsibility of the architect-designer.

*Individual
study units
and carrels*

In libraries, resources centers, learning spaces, and many other places throughout the school, individual study units must be provided. Sometimes these become carrels with or without wiring for reception af audio and video information from remote locations. Carrels need not be more elaborate and more expensive than the functional needs require; often, mock-up carrels can be made in the local shop for experimentation and the final can be made in quantity to meet the local requirements. Again, the carrels should be planned by the designer as an integral part of the environment, and again, a mix of several different types of carrel may be the best answer for a school or college building.

PROJECTION SYSTEMS

*Design of
projection systems*

The display of information by various projection techniques is a basic design factor in educational facilities with new media, and involves far more than the simple provision of projectors and screens. For effective uses of projected media, coordinated projection systems are required; the design of these systems poses some new and and unique problems for architects and planners.

*Two types of
projection systems*

Two basic types of systems may be used—front and rear—and each has desirable and undesirable characteristics. In larger rooms, where room light is necessary during projection, rear projection is generally the best system. In either case, a projection system consists of the best combination of projector, screen, controls, projected material, viewing area and room lighting necessary to accomplish specific learning objectives.

Characteristics of screens and projectors

A tremendous variety of projectors is available in terms of types of projection materials, lumen output, controls, cost, dependability, and the like. Projectors must be selected to meet specific local needs; generally simple, inexpensive equipment is available to perform most tasks. In selecting screens, a number of screen characteristics such as brightness, brightness ratio, contrast ratio, gain, reflection factor, viewing angle, and bend angle, must all be considered in relationship to the characteristics of the projector and the other components of the system. Many types of front and rear projection screens are available, each with its particular set of inherent characteristics.

Controls for equipment and lighting

Equipment controls should be in the hands of the instructor and should be simple and uncomplicated. Remote controls for all equipment will be necessary in the larger rooms and are preferable in the smaller ones. Also, the equipment controls should also control the lighting; when a projector is activated by the instructor, the lights in the room should go to the level of light appropriate for that medium.

Legibility standards

All projected materials that contain symbolic information that must be comprehended should meet basic legibility standards both in terms of contrast ratio and size of letters and numbers.

Determining the viewing area

Finally, the student must be placed in the proper relation to the projection surfaces; this "viewing area" is defined by minimum and maximum viewing distances, and a maximum viewing angle. These factors vary according to the types of projection, the projection material, the screens, and the amount of light in the room. Then, the actual capacity of a room is determined by the type and arrangement of seating placed within the viewing area which is appropriate for a particular set of conditions.

OTHER MEDIA HARDWARE

Complexities of selecting production equipment

Besides the components for projection systems, many other types of equipment must be selected to introduce media into an educational system. The selection of production equipment used in the various production-support centers, regional centers, educational laboratories, and communication centers, requires vast professional experience and advice, and such advice should be sought early in planning if it is not available within the school system or institution. Decisions will be required as to equipment types for television origination, recording and distribution, motion picture filming and processing, audio recording and distribution, and duplication and printing, not to mention assembly, editing, drafting, preview, conference and the dozens of other functions housed in these facilities.

Other hardware
for learning spaces

In the learning spaces other decisions are necessary including the selection of chalkboards, tackboards, TV monitors and receivers, audio distribution systems, student response systems, and audio playback equipment. In the resources facilities, additional equipment ranging from individual projectors and recorders to computer-based information storage and retrieval systems must be selected. All of these decisions require study and evaluation based on performance, economic, and aesthetic criteria.

REPORT **C**

A TECHNICAL GUIDE

 Library of Congress Catalog Card No. 66-25154
Copyright 1966, Center for Architectural Research, Rensselaer Polytechnic Institute
Photos by Carl Howard and Rensselaer's Offices of Institutional Research and
Institute Relations.

EDUCATIONAL FACILITIES WITH NEW MEDIA
REPORT C: A Technical Guide

The final report of an architectural research study conducted by the staff of the Center for Architectural Research, School of Architecture, Rensselaer Polytechnic Institute, Troy, New York, under the terms of contract number OE-316-031 between Rensselaer and the United States Office of Education.

Alan C. Green
M. C. Gassman
Wayne F. Koppes
Raymond D. Caravaty
David S. Haviland

CONTENTS

1 TECHNICAL CONCERNS: AN INTRODUCTION

Learning spaces more complex

One fact is evident; educational facilities planned for the optimum use of media do not look like, and are not designed like, the conventional classrooms of the past. Classrooms were once simple enclosures of space containing students, teacher, chalkboards, desks, and some storage cabinets. Changing educational methods, coupled with the uses of media, have changed not only the form of the classroom, but the way it functions.

Technical guidance

Some technical guidance for design of these new learning spaces is necessary; several general principles should be reviewed.

Change and obsolescence

1. Change is the password in the media field, and obsolescence is the constant fear. Equipment and hardware are undergoing constant modifications and improvements; new kinds of equipment and new models of existing types are coming on the market daily. On the one hand educational administrators are understandably reluctant to invest in projectors, TV equipment and other hardware today that may be obsolete tomorrow, yet the teaching staff recognizes that the educational process and facilities for it cannot perform properly until adequately equipped. Several points may help resolve this dilemma:

Buy only what's needed

- Purchase only the equipment needed immediately and which the faculty is able to use effectively. When the remaining equipment is needed, improved models, possibly at lower prices, will be available.

Buy simple equipment

- Purchase initial equipment that will meet basic functional criteria, but which is simple and uncomplicated in operation and generally less costly than the sophisticated, complex equipment that may be more appropriate for later purchase.

Buy compatible equipment

- Whatever equipment is purchased now should form systems of compatible components, and should permit additional components of equipment to be added later.

Budget for change

- Budgets can reflect a realistic approach to equipment change and obsolescence by providing annual funds specifically for replacement, upgrading and expansion of media systems and components. Institutions should not be put in a position where all equipment for a long time to come has to be provided when the building is first built; some of the funds would better be spent in subsequent years for change.

Planning for later use of media

2. Not only does hardware change, but there is another dimension to to the problem. Many spaces designed and built today will eventually contain media hardware even though uses of media in the spaces are not a design factor for the present. How to plan today's schools to also accommodate tomorrow's hardware is the concern. Some points that may help are:

Design basic space correctly now

- Design the spaces properly now so that equipment can be changed and added later. For instance, if in initial design the proper relationship is established between screens and students, the manner in which images are projected can change without changing the room. The introduction of new projection equipment will not necessitate remodelling the room.

Prior planning can simplify change

- Some prior planning will greatly simplify the later installation of more complex and more extensive systems of equipment. For instance, dropped ceilings, open conduit, and large raceways will accommodate future cables and wiring; access panels and frequent juncture boxes will ease the pulling of cabling; extra initial power service in anticipation of added equipment will eliminate problems of insufficient power; lighting which is installed initially to provide multiple levels will allow the later installation of projection equipment with varying image brightnesses; designing for good acoustical isolation now will prevent problems when media employing recorded sound are introduced later; and installing ductwork and equipment areas now for later air conditioning when added uses of media demand it, will reduce the amount of later construction and remodelling.

Not all equipment built-in

- Much of the hardware subject to change does not need to be built into the fabric of the space, but rather may be left free-standing to facilitate modifications and substitutions.

Use of self-contained cabinets

- Often media can later be introduced into facilities through self-contained cabinets which contain projectors, screens, auxiliary display surfaces, and controls. The "media module"

[handwritten note: hard to do with storage/retrieval]

(see Report B) was developed, in part, to help answer the problem of later incorporating media. However, proper viewing area, lighting, power, and circulation should be provided initially.

Budget for remodelling

● Even with the best of prior planning, later incorporation of media may require some remodelling and construction work. As with equipment, some annual budgeting provisions should be provided to cover these changes in facilities. Minor remodelling to up-date facilities and to allow for expanded and improved uses of media is not necessarily a confession of poor initial planning.

Not everything is subject to obsolescence

3. Some parts of learning spaces are far less vulnerable to change and obsolescence than media equipment. For instance, seating should be selected for durability and ease of maintenance, as well as for functional and aesthetic reasons. Good seating is a sound investment and it should be purchased to last. This is true of storage cabinets and casework and other furniture. Good lighting, allowing several levels, should be provided initially as should proper acoustical treatment and climatic conditioning. Those areas of technology not subject to change should be well provided.

Simplicity the key for teacher usage

4. All apparatus and equipment, all technology, should be designed for simple operation and control. Teachers are generally not technicians and excessive gadgetry and complicated controls will impede the effective uses of media. If one switch will turn on a projector and dim the lights, that is far better than a switch for the projector fan, a switch for the projection lamp, and several rheostats for lighting. This same reasoning applies to all types of classroom lighting, acoustics, climate, and instructional equipment. It also is important when planning and equipping projection areas and studios to be used by teachers. Simplicity is particularly important when teachers and staff have had little previous experience with media. Complexities will turn them away from media, rather than encouraging its use.

Importance of standardization and compatability

5. Standardization and compatability are important in selecting equipment and hardware, in order to simplify maintenance, reduce upkeep costs, and keep down the number of required spare parts. If all 2x2 projectors are the same, rather than many different manufacturers through a district or institution, the savings in time, money and frustration are easy to understand. This is particularly true in selecting television systems and other production equipment. With the growing shortage of technical help qualified to maintain media equipment, standardization and compatability become more and more significant in selecting equipment.

The translation of these general principles on planning the technical aspects are covered more fully in the following discussions.

2 ENVIRONMENT FOR MEDIA: LIGHTING, ACOUSTICS, CLIMATE

*Environment
must meet
physiological
needs*

Certain physiological needs, including seeing, hearing, and bodily comfort, must be met in order for students to learn within man-made environments. The fact that learning media are part of the educational system places some special demands on the environments in which students, media, and instructor gather for learning. The following guidance is offered to help insure that lighting, acoustics, and climate in learning spaces are planned to encourage optimum learning with media.

LIGHTING

*Lighting design
begins early*

The goal for all school lighting is to allow students and instructors to see comfortably and efficiently, and without undue distraction. Although proper school lighting has been a concern for years, still it often happens that too little attention is paid to the requirements of proper lighting during early planning stages. Too frequently the lighting layout is postponed until all other design problems are solved, instead of considering illumination as a basic ingredient of design. When the question of lighting is belatedly considered, it is frequently found that some of the proper locations for lighting fixtures have been pre-empted by a structural member or a ventilating duct, and the quality of illumination must be compromised.

*Lighting and
image viewing*

The provision of proper lighting is of special importance in learning spaces intended for the optimum use of media; it is the type and quality of lighting during the viewing of images that is important. There is a wealth of available information about proper lighting for conventional learning tasks, but much less is known about proper lighting for image viewing.

*Problems of
natural light*

In typical classroom situations, illumination is provided by a combination of natural and artificial sources, and often daylight is a major contributor. For ideal projection conditions, though, daylight is often a disturbing factor to be controlled or eliminated. Many of the smaller spaces in which images are projected will have windows, and where they provide too much ambient light on the screen, they will have to be shaded. In the larger spaces intended for the use of projected media, there should preferably be no windows. Artificial lighting can readily be controlled, and in proper amounts is essential to proper viewing conditions. Therefore, the following will deal primarily with illumination provided by artificial means.

*Lighting as a
tool of design*

In the design of interior spaces particularly, artificial lighting should be considered as one of the essential "tools" of architectural design; it may contribute as much as the choice of materials, finishes, or even the room shape itself.

*Four functions
of lighting*

The four basic functions of lighting are to provide:

Visibility, as influenced by the amount, distribution, color and control provided;

Comfort, as determined by the absence of glare and eye strain;

Atmosphere, as provided by the psychological reactions produced; and

Composition, as seen in its effects upon the architectural surroundings.

Proper lighting of the learning spaces should be designed to fulfill all of these functions.

*Optimum conditions
for viewing media*

Optimum conditions for the viewing of projected media impose two basic requirements in respect to room lighting:

- the provision of appropriate levels and quality of illumination concurrently on the screen, the task surfaces and the surroundings, and

- the proper means and timing of lighting controls.

The typical conventional classroom is deficient on both counts. Usually darkening of the room necessitates lowering the window shades, or placing special blinds, then turning off the lights, and the light switch seldom is located convenient to the projector. Then there is insufficient light for notetaking, and if the presentation is lengthy, drowsiness overtakes many of the viewers.

*Understanding
of terms
important*

In any discussion of lighting the understanding of, and distinction between, certain fundamental technical terms is necessary. Actually we don't see illumination. We see only brightness or light; brightness as reflected from a surface or transmitted through some medium, such as a flame or the sun itself. The light radiating from a source is measured in footcandles; the brightness of a surface, whether due to the reflection or transmission of light, is measured in footlamberts. A lumen is a unit measure of light quantity (luminous energy), and is used in measuring both footcandles and footlamberts. Either one is equal to one lumen per square foot of surface. The essential distinction is that in one case it's light coming from a light source onto the surface (incident light), and in the other, it's light emanating from it, either by reflection or transmission.

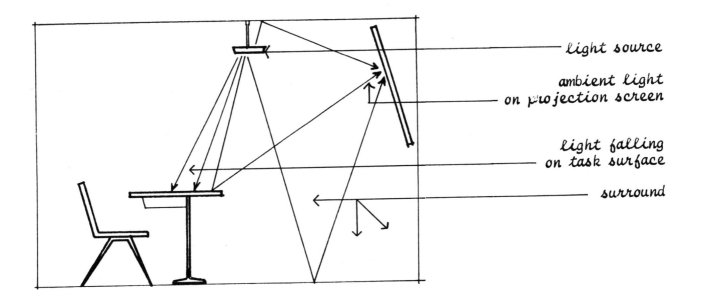

— light source

— ambient light on projection screen

— light falling on task surface

— surround

Brightness ratio and contrast ratio

In the main, it is the brightness of surfaces, and especially the relative brightnesses (brightness ratio) of various surfaces within the field of vision, that are of primary concern. It's important to realize that, contrary to a common concept, brightness does not vary with distance. "Brightness ratio" is a term applied to two relatively large areas; "contrast", a term with a similar meaning, refers to the relative brightness of small adjacent areas, such as printed characters and their background.

Requirements of lighting when projecting

The essential requirements of good lighting for optimum viewing of projected images are chiefly these:

During the projection of images on a screen:

- The student's tablet (or writing) surface should be adequately lighted to facilitate taking notes; it should have as nearly as possible the same brightness as the average brightness of the projected image.

- The light falling on this tablet surface should not produce shadows, and the seated student should not be aware of room light sources within his normal line of vision.

- The brightness of other visual task surfaces, such as chalkboards and displays, when in use, should also be about the same as that of the projected image. When not in use, their surface brightness should be lower, to blend inconspicuously with the general background.

- Other surfaces within the viewer's vision, including chalkboards and display areas not in use, should be less bright, but their brightness should not be less than 1/10 that of the average screen brightness.

Requirements otherwise

When no projection of images is taking place:

- The general level of room lighting should be consistent with typical classroom lighting.

- In the large rooms, supplementary local lighting should be provided on chalkboards, display surfaces, demonstration areas, and the instructor himself, as may be required.

- Projection screens not in use should be inconspicuous.

Lighting of pre-set levels should be controlled by the instructor, or "tied-in" with projection equipment. In the interest of economy, these lighting conditions should be achieved without the use of elaborate and expensive dimmer devices, custom fixtures or other costly equipment.

*Various media
need various
lighting
levels*

In short, the goal in order to minimize eyestrain is the acheivement of proper relationships between the brightness of the screen image and other task surfaces and surrounding surfaces within the viewer's field of vision. This is somewhat complicated by the fact that the reference brightness value—the average screen brightness—is not constant. With any projected media, it depends on number of variable factors such as the lumen output of the projector, the type of screen used, and the nature of the projected material. Also, the characteristic average brightness of screen image produced by various media differ even more significantly. It would be highly impractical to attempt to accommodate all of these varying brightness levels. But it is advisable to provide several levels of room lighting which are consistent with, and keyed to, the medium being used.

*Large rooms
have greater
problems*

The lighting requirements become more critical, and consequently the lighting system becomes more complex, as the size of the learning space increases. In the smaller rooms, conventional ceiling light sources are generally satisfactory for providing two levels and sufficient background lighting of wall and ceiling surfaces is usually provided by "spill" from these sources. In the larger rooms, though, it is usually advisable to provide supplementary special "wash" lighting on the wall areas to bring their brightness up to the proper level in respect to the screen brightness.

*Avoid ambient
light*

It is vitally important in all cases that the room lighting be so directed that as little as possible reaches the projection screen itself. Ambient light on the screen tends to "wash out" the projected image, and its effect becomes more critical as the average screen brightness decreases. Thus, it is particularly important in the larger rooms that projection screens be shielded from stray room lighting.

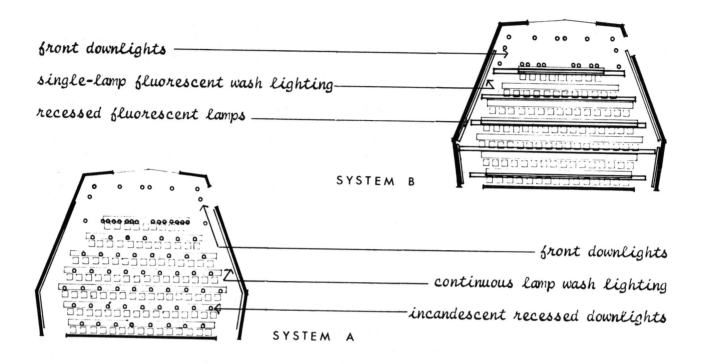

front downlights

single-lamp fluorescent wash lighting

recessed fluorescent lamps

SYSTEM B

front downlights

continuous lamp wash lighting

incandescent recessed downlights

SYSTEM A

Two types of systems for large group

For larger spaces two basic types of systems are possible. System A uses incandescent recessed downlights located in the ceiling over the seating area, with auxiliary lighting of the side walls by means of a continuous band of lamps mounted on the wall behind an opaque fascia strip. The whole system is controlled at predetermined levels by means of dimmers. System B consists of recessed fluorescent troffers placed in continuous rows across the ceiling paralleling the seating rows, with a directional 45° cut-off, parabolic reflector grid located below the luminaires and flush with the ceiling. Another line of single-lamp troffers with similar reflector grids is placed in the ceiling along each side wall to provide wash lighting on the walls. This system does not require dimmer controls; instead, several lighting levels can be provided by circuitry and switching. In both systems, accent lighting of the display surfaces, chalkboards, demonstration area and instructor's station can be provided by units recessed in the ceiling. Both systems could be completely controlled from the instructor's station by automatic switching tied-in with the projector controls.

Choice of a system

Naturally there are modifications and combinations of these two systems that would perform satisfactorily. The choice must be made by weighing factors such as initial and operating costs, maintenance costs, reliability, operating noise, and quality of desired light.

Importance of
color and
texture

In providing appropriate surface brightnesses, the choice of colors and textures is a most important consideration. The writing surfaces (desk or counter tops) should be neither glossy white, producing glare, nor a dark color, contrasting with the writing paper, but should have a light-colored matte finish with a light reflection value of 50 to 60%. The floor, ceiling and walls may be generally light colored, but near the projection screens, they may be darker to minimize the amount of light they reflect on the screens. Chalkboards should have low reflectance to provide good contrast for chalk. The use of bright metal trim anywhere in the room is distracting and objectionable, and should by all means be avoided.

Lighting
controls

Appropriate lighting levels should be predetermined and preset, and the instructor's control should extend only to the selection of sequence and duration. It is recommended that when a lectern is used, as in the larger spaces, the lighting circuits be so arranged that they are controlled by the same switches which operate the projectors, so that the switch activating the projector also automatically reduces the level of room lighting, and the switch turning it off automatically raises the room lighting to its normal level. In the smaller rooms lighting will be controlled by simple wall switches, or may be part of the controls built into media modules.

ACOUSTICS

Acoustics a
concern in all
buildings

Architectural acoustics has long been a matter of concern in concert halls and large auditoria, but only recently has good acoustics in nearly all types of buildings become a concern. With the rising noise level of our modern environment, there is increasing concern with noise control problems, and now acoustical requirements are even being introduced into building codes.

Education
depends on
communication

Good acoustics are, of course, important in school buildings. Education depends on communication; good hearing conditions are just as essential as good lighting, and both must be carefully considered early in the planning stage. The growing interest in school building acoustics has, in fact, led to many special studies and investigations. Two developments in particular have prompted this concern: the introduction of open planning and the increasing use of electronic media in teaching. Both of these developments are highly significant, and both complicate the "noise problem". Unfortunately, as they affect acoustics, they are basically incompatible.

*Special problems
when using media*

The fundamentals of acoustics for school buildings are fairly common knowledge; however, it is important to call attention to the essential acoustical features of spaces intended specifically for new media, and to indicate how the basic theory of acoustics affects their design. The use of electronic media is an underlying concern, but the merits of spatial flexibility are also recognized. The implications of both are of special interest.

*Two objective
of acoustics*

Architectural acoustics should recognize two objectives:

- the provision of good hearing conditions wherever desired, and

- the elimination, as far as possible, of unwanted sound or noise

Both are important in school design, but not necessarily of equal importance in all spaces. This depends upon the intended function of the space.

Hearing Conditions

*Factors
affecting
hearing*

Hearing conditions within a room or space depend upon the size and shape of the room, the location and volume of sound, and the disposition of sound-absorbing and sound-reflecting surfaces within the the room. The sound heard at any point within confined space consists of direct sound from the sound source, plus an infinite sequence of sound reflections from surrounding surfaces. The sound level of these reflections—the reverberant sound—depends upon whether the surroundings—the walls, floor, ceiling and furnishings—absorb or reflect the sound. Good hearing conditions are achieved by the control of sound reflection and absorption, and this, in turn, involves several basic requirements:

- the reinforcement, as necessary, of the sound source by reflective surfaces

- the avoidance of long-delayed reflections from remote hard surfaces

- the elimination of inter-reflections (flutter) between parallel hard surfaces

- the control of the persistance of sound (reverberation)

- the control of background noise within the room

*Problems
vary with
size of rooms*

Good hearing conditions are obviously essential in all spaces where the learning process requires listening. Listening is essential in learning rooms of all sizes, from the small conference rooms to large auditoria, but good hearing conditions are seldom a problem to achieve in smaller spaces. As the size of the space increases, so also does the importance of acoustical design, and the proper planning of large spaces may require the assistance of acoustical experts.

*Small and
medium size
rooms*

Surface treatments and finishes in small rooms have relatively little effect on hearing conditions. In the medium group spaces accommodating up to 60 persons, it will generally suffice to provide a peripheral area of absorptive material on all sides of the room except that occupied by the instructor. A major part of the ceiling area should be hard and reflective to reinforce the instructor's voice or other sound source.

*Large rooms
cause
biggest
problems*

In the larger group spaces, the disposition of reflective and absorptive surfaces, including the shape of the room itself, becomes increasingly important as the room dimensions and the distances sound must travel become larger. The objective should always be to so dispose these materials within the room that occupants do not receive perceptibly delayed repetitions of sound. If the surfaces lining the room are hard, and therefore sound-reflective, sound waves are bounced back and forth many times before they die out, and a long "reverberation period" results. When large areas of porous, and therefore sound-absorbent material such as carpet, upholstered furniture or special acoustical "blankets" are introduced, the reflective energy is greatly reduced. Sound is largely absorbed and dies away quickly; the reverberation period is greatly reduced.

*Acoustical
facts of life*

These acoustical "facts of life" have important design implications. They dictate that surfaces relatively close to the sound source should be reflective to amplify and disperse the sound, while surfaces behind the audience, facing the sound source, should be absorptive to minimize reflection and reverberation. The provision, in

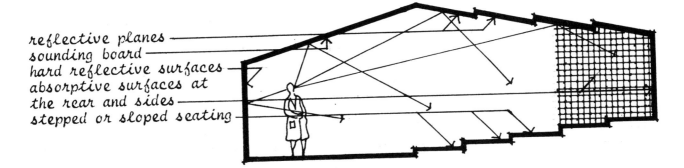

reflective planes
sounding board
hard reflective surfaces
absorptive surfaces at
the rear and sides
stepped or sloped seating

effect, of an inclined "sounding board" surface over the instructor's area is essential, and may often be provided by the conformation of the ceiling itself. As a rule, other ceiling surfaces, too, should be reflective, flat planes. Curved surfaces, particularly domes, should be avoided, because they focus, rather than disperse sound. Non-parallel side walls, converging in the direction of the sound source, are preferred, because they improve the dispersion of sound and tend to reduce the reverberation period.

Good sight lines, good hearing lines

As the room size increases, the conformation of the floor area becomes important for acoustical reasons as well as for viewing. Sloped or stepped floors in the larger spaces improve the general hearing conditions, because sound from the front of the room is better dispersed to all members of the audience. It's important to remember that good sight lines mean good "hearing lines".

Sound Systems

Generally amplification of voice unnecessary

Under normal conditions, amplification systems should not be necessary in most of the facilities illustrated in Report B, if the recommendations as to room shape and acoustical treatment are followed. Exceptions will occur in the large rooms where it may be advisable to provide means of reinforcing live speech because of the likely limitations of some speakers. In all of the learning spaces, though, electronically reproduced sounds will be used and facilities should be provided for their distribution. With a built-in sound system being required anyway, it may be desirable in the larger rooms to design it to be used also for amplification and distribution of live sounds. In all cases, there should be only one sound system in any learning space, and it should be capable of accommodating interchangeably all needs—sound tracks on films, audio tapes, radio, television audio, intercom announcements, and, when desired, sounds picked up by room microphones.

Two types of sound system

For the larger rooms, two types of sound systems are available: 1) distributed, low level systems, with speakers located at various points in the ceiling, and 2) central, high level systems, with a single speaker (or battery of speakers) located at a point above the instructional area and directed at the center of the audience. The selection will depend on the size and functions of the space; both are represented in the design studies.

Quality of sound important

A minimum requirement of any sound system is that it have sufficient reproduction quality for full intelligibility. In most of the rooms music will frequently be reproduced, and in certain rooms this may be the chief function of the system. The tonal quality of the system then becomes of prime importance. It's essential in all cases, too, that uniform volume be provided throughout the listening area with no feedback. When used to amplify live speech, it's important that the amplified sound seems to be coming from the same source as the direct live sound.

Analyze long term costs when selecting equipment

Reliability and low maintenance cost of the equipment deserve more consideration than they often receive. If a useful life of from 15 to 20 years without major overhaul is expected, then overall costs, including probable servicing, repairs and replacements should be the governing consideration in selecting the system components, rather than initial costs only. The cheaper installations often prove to be the most expensive purchases in the long run.

Sound Isolation

Amplified sound versus open planning

For reasons previously indicated, the problems of sound isolation between spaces are probably more urgent—and more difficult—in today's schools than are those related to the direction of sound originating within the listening area itself. The expanding use of reproduced sounds calls for improved sound barriers, while at the same time the search for spatial freedom and flexibility encourages the elimination of substantial space dividers. Unfortunately, the invisible sound barrier is yet to be invented and some logical compromise solution is necessary.

Three factors determine quietness

Three principal factors determine the "quietness" of an enclosed space in respect to air-borne sounds:

- the level of sound (noise) in adjacent spaces

- the sound insulation quality of the intervening space enclosure, and

- the level of background noise within the space itself.

It is the relationship of these factors that determines the degree of acoustical comfort experienced in a room. For many years the importance of the sound insulating value (or transmission loss) of walls and floors has been recognized; it's only recently that the significance of background noise has received much attention.

Mass and stiffness of partitions

Sound isolation from outside sources can be provided either by distance or by enclosure. Within a building sound isolation must be provided by floors and partitions, and it's in the construction of partitions that most problems of isolating air-borne sounds arise. The sound—isolating properties of a barrier are determined largely by the mass and inertia of the barrier material. Mass is important, but mass alone is not a dependable measure. Stiffness, or rather the lack of it, may be even more important. A partition consisting of gypsum board on both sides of wood studs which are saw-split to reduce their stiffness, is a better sound barrier than a plastered 6'' cinder block wall which weighs almost three times as much.

Partitions must not leak sound

To be totally effective, any sound barrier must be air-tight. Even the smallest openings, such as open joints or cracks, electrical outlet boxes back to back, or keyholes, will greatly reduce the sound—isolating value of a partition. All openings are sound leaks, and have even more significance, relatively, than leaks in waterproofing. A hole of only one square inch in 100 square feet of wall having a 40—decibel transmission loss rating will "leak" as much sound as all the rest of the wall.

Improved flexible partitions

It is because of a combination of deficiencies,—light mass, stiffness and most importantly, numerous leaks,—that until recently most reasonable priced flexible or folding partitions have been relatively ineffective as sound barriers. In the past several years, however, this situation has improved. Some manufacturers have developed new products which are better designed and engineered, with careful attention to a better choice of materials and thorough edge sealing, resulting in greatly improved acoustical performance.

Distractions of recorded sound in open planning

In some of the newer schools, open planning has been used extensively with no full partitions separating classrooms or corridors. Proponents of such planning claim that the liberal use of carpeting, acoustical surfacing and baffles, can overcome noise problems. Studies have been made to evaluate this approach to school planning, emphasizing its psychological advantages and attempting to rationalize its acoustical disadvantages. Significantly, although the majority of teachers interviewed appear to find the spaces generally quite acceptable, many of them stated that the use of television, or record playing in adjoining areas is distracting.

Conclusions

General experience, reinforced by such studies as these, has led to several important conclusions:

- The omission of full and substantial partitions between learning spaces limits the proper and effective use of electronic media. Open planning of this type (without full partitions) may be acceptable for some teaching–learning situations, particularly among young children, where a high level of background noise can be tolerated. It cannot be recommended where electronic media are to be regularly used, unless headsets or low volume speakers are employed.

- The minimum acceptable sound barrier between spaces planned for the regular use of electronic media, as in this study, should have a transmission loss of not less than 40 decibels.

Reduce other noises

Background noise level within the learning space itself must also be reduced below objectionable levels. The more commonly disturbing sources are mechanical ventilation equipment and projection equipment.

Enclose projection equipment

It is recommended that an enclosure be provided for all projectors to minimize their noise. In smaller rooms, such enclosures may be simply boxes or "media modules" containing the equipment. Interior surfaces of these enclosures should be lined with sound-absorbent material.

Front and rear projection areas

In the larger rooms, front projection equipment should be housed in permanent "soundproof" projection booths. Projection should be through a glazed panel, rather than open ports, and the glazing should be heavy plate glass set in resilient gasketing. Rear projection spaces for the large rooms must also be carefully designed to confine equipment noise. The projection screen will be vulnerable to sound leakage. If a rigid screen is used, it should be set in resilient mountings. The typical flexible screen has inadequate value as a sound barrier, and should be backed up with a plate glass panel sealed with a resilient compound or gasket. Both types of projection areas should contain sound-absorbent material, and any doors connecting it with the learning space should be of solid construction and gasketed.

These guidelines for designing acoustically satisfactory facilities with media are only useful if followed early in the design process. Good acoustics cannot be achieved as an afterthought.

CLIMATE

*Importance of
proper climate*

The optimum learning environment is more than simply a physically comfortable climate; it is a climate which encourages learning,—an atmosphere in which the student is alert and attentive. The need for such an atmosphere is particularly essential in spaces where media are being extensively used. In these spaces, the provision of a climate conducive to alert attention is as essential as proper lighting and acoustics; temperature, humidity and air movement should all be carefully controlled.

*Providing for
air-conditioning*

Air conditioning in schools, though a relatively recent innovation, is rapidly becoming common practice in new construction. With more and more schools in all parts of the country anticipating the eventual adoption of a year-round program, it seems that few schools should be built without at least making provision for air conditioning. This will facilitate providing the ideal environment in learning spaces with media throughout the school. Of the schools in use today, however, relatively few are air conditioned. Many of these non-airconditioned schools will be altered and renovated to provide large group learning spaces.

To meet the environmental requirements of these spaces it will be advisable, if not mandatory, to install special air conditioning equipment to serve them.

*Special characteristics
of large spaces*

In general, the climate conditioning of facilities with media poses no unique technical problems, although the need for conditioning and the complexity of the problem increases with the size of the room. In designing the mechanical equipment for the larger group spaces, special attention should be given to the implications of these characteristic conditions:

1. The number of occupants will be relatively large.

2. Many of the rooms will have no windows.

3. Lighting levels, and therefore the heat output from lighting, will vary.

4. Good hearing conditions are mandatory, necessitating careful control of equipment noises.

Even in typical classrooms, cooling...

It is generally known that even in typical school classrooms, more cooling than heating is usually required when outside temperatures are above 25°F, and that good school climate control requires less attention to heating than to cooling in all seasons of the year, regardless of geographic location. Because of the relatively dense population, the high level of artificial illumination, and the often generous use of window glass in typical classrooms, the most common complaints have to do with overheating and poor ventilation. Each occupant contributes about 300 Btu's of heat per hour, and heat is given off by lighting and electrical apparatus at the rate of about 3.4 Btu's per watt per hour. In rooms without windows, where there is much less heat loss through the walls, the need for cooling rather than heating is of course even more prevalent.

...rather than heating, is the problem

Without question, then, the dominant temperature control problem in the larger learning spaces will be that of cooling, when the room is in use. When not in use—off periods, over night and weekends—some heating will likely be required during the normal heating season. In many of these rooms varying levels of lighting, from 5 to 60+ Ft.C. will be used during teaching periods; the maintenance of a proper room temperature under the fluctuating heat output from lighting will be required. In the smaller rooms, portable projectors and other equipment will often be used and they will be significant sources of heat. Projection equipment for the larger rooms will be isolated in separate spaces which have their own ventilation.

Relative humidity also a factor

Humidity, too, must be controlled within an appropriate range, but relative humidity has less significance in providing the proper climate than do temperature and ventilation. Whereas at one time a minimum relative humidity of 50% was generally recommended, engineers now consider a range of from 30% to 55% quite acceptable. To prevent exceeding this top value, it is frequently necessary to provide dehumidification, to remove the moisture given off by the occupants through evaporation.

Importance of proper ventilation

Ventilation will always be required just as it is in most conventional classrooms. Research has established that the chief function of ventilation air is not to replace oxygen or control the carbon dioxide content, as is often assumed, but to dilute body odors which become intensified in densely occupied spaces. Usually, when there are complaints about poor ventilating, it is the "stale odor" that's found objectionable. Odors may be controlled by several means, but in school buildings they are usually dispelled by dilution with fresh air. This "fresh" air need not necessarily all be outdoor air, however. Recirculated room air that has been cleansed of odors will serve the purpose; its use usually reduces the cost of the ventilating system.

Amounts of ventilation

The amount of ventilation needed to maintain proper oxygen content and limit the carbon dioxide content to a healthy minimum is only about 4 cubic feet per minute per person, but the amount required to dilute odors is much larger, varying with the number of cubic feet of room volume provided per occupant. For sedentary adults, a minimum of 25 cubic feet of fresh air should be provided per person in small, crowded spaces (100 cubic feet of volume per person); in larger, uncrowded spaces (400 to 500 cubic feet of volume per person) this may be as little as 7 cubic feet per occupant. For moderate activity, these amounts should be increased by 50%. Thus the minimum amount of fresh air to be supplied in the larger and medium-sized learning spaces will probably range from 10 to 15 cfm per person, depending on the age of the students. Cooling requirements, however, as opposed to ventilation requirements, will often necessitate introducing larger volumes of air.

*Cost of heating
fresh air*

It should be noted that introducing an oversupply of outdoor ventilating air during the heating season, when this air has to be heated even for cooling purposes, may add significantly to fuel costs and should therefore be avoided. In one study made of two similar schools in Ohio, one of which provided about three times as much outdoor ventilation air as the other, the difference in fuel costs attributable to this factor was over 60%.

*Planning air
movement*

Air movement is a basic essential to the proper learning environment. Sufficient air circulation should be provided over the surface of the body to carry away the layer of warm, moist air covering the skin, but it must be provided in such a way as to avoid noticeable drafts. In the larger rooms, at least, it will probably be advisable to introduce air at or near the ceiling and exhaust it at a low level. Return air grilles should be so located that the air flow is reasonably uniform over the seating area, and will probably be placed either in the side walls near the floor or, in rooms with stepped floors, may be in the riser faces under the seats. If sufficient in number and size, there will be no objectionable drafts.

*Mixing systems
required*

Ventilation will be needed at all times, but temperatures must be held constant. A controlled combination of cooling and heating is required which must be quickly responsive to varying thermal loads within the rooms. There are several types of ductwork and fan systems which can be used to meet these fluctuating requirements. The most flexible would be a double duct system, in which air is carried at different temperatures in two parallel ducts. It would be an advantage to have closed loops formed by the ducts, so that there are two paths for air at any point. In this way a change in demand can be handled without causing excessive disturbance in the friction drop of the ductwork. Mixing boxes connecting to two ducts would draw air from each as determined by thermostats operating controls at the mixing box.

Avoid sounds being carried through ducts

Because good hearing conditions are mandatory in all of the learning spaces, it is imperative that great care be taken in laying out ductwork and in selecting fans, blowers and other equipment. Ducts must be located and routed to avoid carrying sounds from room to room. This will be a matter of particular concern where amplified sound can be carried readily and distinctly through ductwork. If a double duct mixing-box system is used, individual runs from the box should be lined with sound-absorbing material. This is a most important caution.

Isolate equipment

In selecting the mechanical equipment itself, the rated noise levels should be carefully examined and verified, to insure that the noise introduced into the learning space from this source will not exceed the desirable masking level. In most cases this will necessitate locating the equipment at some distance from the rooms it serves, where it can be acoustically isolated, and if necessary, lining the connecting ducts with sound-absorbent material to minimize sound transmission.

3 ENVIRONMENT FOR MEDIA: FURNITURE

*Planning furniture
an integral part
of the design process*

For effective uses of media in education, the manner which class-rooms, seminar rooms, independent study facilities and other learning spaces are furnished is an important design decision. Unfortunately, too often the selection and purchase of furniture are left until too late in the planning process when energies, funds and professional services have been expended. Furniture, as part of the learning environment, should be considered an integral part of any space in which media are to be employed; its selection should be based on careful study and professional advice early in planning. Most importantly, functional, aesthetic, and economic criteria should be established during the programming stages when the functional requirements of the spaces are spelled out.

*Fixed seating —
continuous counters
with fixed seats*

Many types of seating for learning spaces are available, but their individual appropriateness varies from space to space. Of the three basic types of seating (fixed, moveable, and combined) fixed has had the advantage of guaranteeing that, once properly positioned, every student will always be in the proper relationship to screens and other display surfaces. Of the various types of fixed seating, the continuous counter with individual fixed chairs provides a desir-able surface for writing and for holding references. This is partic-ularly important in secondary and higher education where the learning process may require extensive use of various types of materials and resources during a class. Also, a continuous counter works well when portable, audio-visual equipment, small demonstrations, or various forms of teaching machines are to be used by students at their seats, or when student response systems, requiring the use of a response panel at each station, are to be installed initially or planned for later installation. This type of seating does require more floor area per unit than most other types of fixed seating, but this may be compensated for by the provision of cross-aisles between each row of seating, allowing students to move freely to and from their seats.

Fixed seating —
theater types

There are many so-called "theater-type" of fixed seating employing a seat with a folding or lifting individual writing surface. Unfortunately, many of the tablet arms provided with this type of seating have the disadvantage of being too small to accommodate writing and reference materials. Lately, some improvements in seating have resulted in folding tablet arms that are adequate in size. Generally, fixed seating of this kind requires less floor area than the continuous counters, but student access to his individual seat is more limited. Also, the necessary moving parts to raise and lower the tablet arms can create maintenance and upkeep problems. Installation of response devices and outlets for equipment can be handled in seating with moveable tablet arms, but this again introduces maintenance problems.

Moveable seating

Moveable seating also introduces a variety of alternatives, and again the provision of an adequate writing surface is extremely important. In rooms where regrouping of students is important, separate table units or seat-table units that are modular to allow conference and discussion groupings are deisrable. Moveable seating mitigates against the use of any individual student instructional device requiring wiring such as response systems, portable recorders or projectors, and power operated teaching machines. Particularly with moveable seating, seating should be scaled and designed with the age and character of the students in mind.

Combined seating

Combined seating is basically of one type—continuous counter with loose seats. This type has the advantages of flexibility, accommodation to many body postures, and reduced cost over the continuous counter with fixed seats. However, for continental seating, the interpretation of building codes may prohibit this type of seating in large rooms. The accompanying diagram illustrates several of the fixed and combined types of seating that are available, together with the average size of writing surfaces and the floor area required.

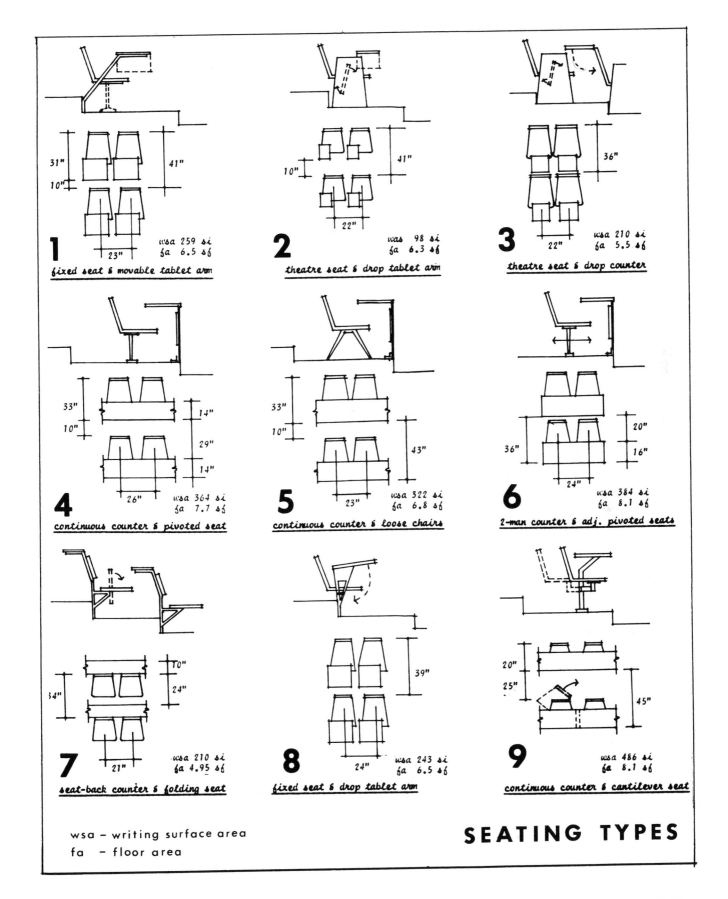

1 fixed seat & movable tablet arm — 31", 10", 41", 23" — wsa 259 si, fa 6.5 sf

2 theatre seat & drop tablet arm — 10", 41", 22" — was 98 si, fa 6.3 sf

3 theatre seat & drop counter — 36", 22" — wsa 210 si, fa 5.5 sf

4 continuous counter & pivoted seat — 33", 10", 14", 29", 14", 26" — wsa 364 si, fa 7.7 sf

5 continuous counter & loose chairs — 33", 10", 43", 23" — wsa 322 si, fa 6.8 sf

6 2-man counter & adj. pivoted seats — 36", 20", 16", 24" — wsa 384 si, fa 8.1 sf

7 seat-back counter & folding seat — 34", 10", 24", 21" — wsa 210 si, fa 4.95 sf

8 fixed seat & drop tablet arm — 39", 24" — wsa 243 si, fa 6.5 sf

9 continuous counter & cantilever seat — 20", 25", 45" — wsa 486 si, fa 8.1 sf

wsa – writing surface area
fa – floor area

SEATING TYPES

*A mix of seating
is often the answer*

In many instances, several types of seating in one space may best meet functional needs. For instance, loose tables and chairs on a flat floor area at the front of a large teaching room can be used for case studies, moot courts, and other instructional methods, while the remainder of the seating is fixed on a sloped/stepped floor. Also, in rooms requiring raised seating, rows of seating may alternate between riser-mounted and floor-mounted types. Particularly in medium group spaces, various types of loose seating may meet the varying requirements dictated by multi-age, multi-class, and non-graded approaches to learning.

*Importance of
good sight lines
from all seats*

Certainly in rooms where projected media are to be used extensively, good sight lines from all seats to all screens are important. Where 40 or more students are involved, this will generally require stepped or sloped floors. However, steep slopes such as seen for years in college lecture halls or amphitheaters are not always necessary. These slopes have usually been dictated by a functional requirement that every student be able to see the top of a demonstration table at the front of the room. Rather than thus increasing the volume of the room, and the cost of the room, electronic means of magnification should be employed which shifts the functional requirement from viewing a demonstration table to the more easily accommodated viewing of screens. By offsetting the rows of seating, and by using platforms containing two rows of seating each, the volume of the room can be reduced without impairing the viewing of screens and information display surfaces.

*Investigate the
the advantages of
continental seating*

In laying out seating in the larger rooms, continental seating which allows cross-aisles between the rows of seats, should be explored. This arrangement can move aisles outside the viewing area, can allow longer rows of seats, and can permit students to move to and from their seats without disturbing other students. The square footage per seating unit based on the total room area may not be much greater than that for more conventional arrangements. Each such solution must be judged in accordance with the applicable building code.

*Criteria and
the method of
selecting
seating*

The selection of seating for each space in an educational building requires the early development of specific criteria against which each alternative is judged. The following outline of criteria may be helpful:

- functional values—writing surface, book storage, comfort and posture, adjustability, accessibility.

- structural values—durability, simplicity of construction.

- ease of cleaning.

- economy of space.

- appearance

- cost

In conjunction with these criteria, a rating method for comparing various seating types was established and is described in the following chart.

CRITERIA FOR SEATING

FUNCTIONAL VALUES

Writing surface: points for size and convenient location of surface. Surfacing material considered in comparing specific designs:

    maximum score...............14 points
    minimum score............... 6 points
    no surface at all.......... 0 points

Book storage: points for adequate and convenient space in addition to writing surface:

    maximum score............... 5 points
    minimum score............... 2 points
    no storage at all.......... 0 points

Adjustability: points for being able to adjust distance between writing surface and seat, and seat and floor; adequacy of legroom and knee-room:

    maximum score............... 6 points
    minimum if ample legroom
      but no adjustment........ 3 points
    minimum score............... 0 points

Accessibility: ease of occupying and vacating seat and using writing surface without disturbing neighbors:

    maximum score............... 9 points
    minimum score............... 3 points

STRUCTURAL VALUES

Durability: points for strength, ruggedness of design, sturdiness of floor attachment, invulnerability to damage:

    maximum score...............12 points
    minimum score............... 4 points

Mechanical simplicity: points for lack of complex mechanisms and moving parts which increase costs of maintenance and repairs:

    maximum score...............10 points
    minimum score............... 3 points

EASE OF CLEANING

Cleaning floor: points for minimum interference of supports or attachments with cleaning the floor:

    maximum score............... 7 points
    minimum score............... 0 points

Cleaning total unit: points for minimum time and effort required for cleaning seat and writing surface:

    maximum score............... 5 points
    minimum score............... 2 points

ECONOMY OF SPACE

points for smallness of floor space required per unit:

    maximum score...............10 points
    minimum score............... 4 points

APPEARANCE

points for cleanliness and attractiveness of the design:

    maximum score...............10 points
    minimum score............... 0 points

COST

points for economy of installed unit:

    maximum score...............12 points
    minimum, if in normal
      cost range............... 5 points
    minimum, if exhorbitant... 0 points

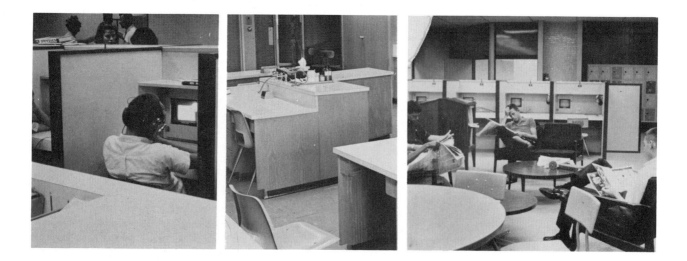

*Selection of other
furniture types
requires careful
analysis and search*

Besides seating, many other kinds of furniture must be designed or selected to complete the furnishings of a learning environment with media. Again, these decisions should be made early and with professional help, the furniture should be considered as an integral part of the space, and the selection should be based on established criteria of function, aesthetics and cost. Storage cabinets, work counters, work areas with utilities, laboratory equipment, teachers stations and lecterns, and many other types of special furniture may be custom designed and built for the particular job, or may be picked from stock, catalog items. In any case, a modular approach based on a dimensional system should be encouraged to simplify detailing and to permit rearrangement of the furniture elements. It would be impossible to review here all the types of furniture involved; it is strongly recommended that an extensive search and review of all available types be made before making final selections.

*Media module
as a piece of
furniture*

One new type of furniture that may be considered in small and medium size rooms is the self-contained cabinet for media or "media module". Here, projector, screen, mirrors and controls are fitted together to form a projection system inside a cabinet; the total unit may be fixed, portable, or a combination of fixed cabinet and portable projector. The media module has been described in detail in Report B; here it should be recognized as one more kind of furniture that should be considered and which can introduce media into new or remodelled facilities.

*Independent
study units*

One major category of furniture should be further mentioned. Independent study units will be found in resource centers and classrooms, and will be related to many other types of spaces. As has been stressed before, these units may be of many types ranging from simple, but comfortable, tables and chairs to complex carrels which provide for the reception of audio and video information. Included are many types of simple study carrels and even comfortable lounge chairs for "soft reading". Often, a mix of all these types will best meet functional needs of an educational plant.

*Simple carrels
may be best*

Student study carrels often seem to be more elaborate and more expensive than functional needs require. Simple carrels may be provided now which can be modified later to permit electronic reception of audio and video. Finally, experimental or mock-up carrels can be designed and built locally for trial and evaluation before a large investment is made in the final answer. The whole field of independent study is undergoing such extensive study and change that a large investment in one solution now may not be appropriate.

4 HARDWARE FOR MEDIA: PROJECTION SYSTEMS

*Importance of
designing systems*

Too frequently the hardware used in audio-visual presentations is regarded as a collection of individual items—a projector, a screen and a speaker—each performing its function more or less independently. A much broader concept is essential if media are to be used with maximum effectiveness. Not only these hardware items, but also the seating area and the environment itself must be considered as integrated components of a system, each influenced by, and depending on all of the others. in producing the total effect. None of these components, even the hardware, can be selected on its merits alone.

*Four factors
influence
viewing conditions*

Regardless of the projected material or method, the effectiveness of the presentation depends upon the ease with which the viewers receive the message. With any normal audience, the quality of viewing conditions is chiefly determined by four factors:

- the appropriateness and efficiency of the projection equipment and screens

- the quality of the projected material

- the location of the viewer in relation to the screen

- the visual and auditory environment

*Objective of
this section*

The chief concern here is to outline the inter-relationships and major considerations affecting the choice of the projection hardware—projector, screen and controls—and to discuss briefly certain criteria for projected materials, and how the optimum viewing area is determined. The visual and auditory environment has been discussed previously; only its influence on the design of projection systems will be covered here.

FRONT AND REAR PROJECTION

*Two types
of projection...*

Before considering any of the above matters, it is important to recognize that two different methods may be used for projecting images onto a screen, and that the choice of method will influence the design of a projection system. These two methods are:

- Front projection, in which both the projector and the viewers are on the same side of an opaque screen which reflects the image, and,

- Rear projection, in which the projector and the viewers are on opposite sides of a translucent screen upon which the image is displayed.

Both methods are employed in the studies presented in Report B. Either one may be used for any type of projector, including the TV projector, but customarily the overhead and opaque projectors are used only in front projection.

*..and their
advantages and
disadvantages*

Both front and rear projection have their inherent advantages and disadvantages, which become clear by comparing them in respect to the most important areas of difference. These are:

- the effect of ambient light,

- space requirements, and

- interference with the projected image.

*Rear projection
allows higher
light levels*

*not presently
agreed to.*

The ambient light level in the room is much more critical with front projection than with rear projection. This means that with present equipment a much higher level of room lighting can be tolerated in the viewing area when rear projection is employed. This is considered to be the chief advantage of rear projection, particularly in larger rooms. In rooms where small image sizes are appropriate, ambient light effects may not be critical providing proper equipment is used. Current developments in the improvement of equipment indicate that the size of acceptable images possible with front projection under useful levels of ambient light will be increased.

*More space for
rear projection*

An undeniable disadvantage of rear projection is that additional space behind the screen must be provided to accommodate the projectors and their throw distances. To conserve space, projectors with short focal length lenses are desirable and mirrors may be used to "bend" the projection rays. Also self-contained screen-projector

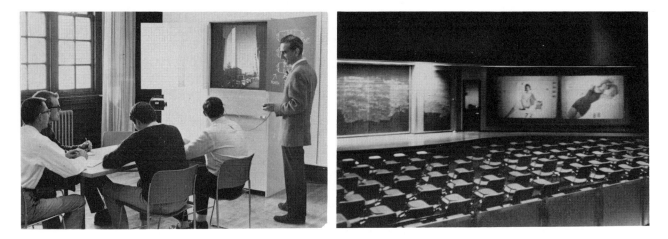

units or media modules may be used. It must be recognized, however, that shortening the focal length of the projector decreases the width of optimum viewing areas, and the use of mirrors generally diminishes the effective brightness of the projected image.

No problems of interference with rear projection

One of the important advantages of rear projection is that the projection rays are protected from interference by either the instructor or the viewers. The instructor can stand in front of the image to point out details without casting shadows. With front projection this is impossible; distracting shadows are cast by any object or person in the path of the projection beam, and the freedom of the instructor is limited accordingly.

Other factors

It has been assumed that in both methods the projectors are located in reasonably soundproof enclosures and that remote control is provided for the instructor who remains at the front of the class. Such assumptions are frequently not valid for front projection, however. With relatively small groups of viewers, portable front projection equipment is often used, and the instructor himself may operate the projector. Used in this way, front projection has several additional disadvantages which should be recognized. Unless precautions are taken to minimize it, the noise of the projector is distractive to viewers, and if the instructor must double as an operator, his effectiveness as a teacher is necessarily diminished.

SCREENS

Screen type important for visual comfort

The design of any projection system must necessarily recognize "the human factor"—the needs and limitations of the observer. The impact and effectiveness of the image displayed largely depends on such matters as its brightness, its legibility and its contrast values.

The human eye can tolerate and adjust to a remarkably wide range of conditions, but if eye strain is to be avoided, these critical variables must be controlled within established limits of acceptability. The projection screen is a major component in determining visual comfort.

A variety of screen types are available for both front and rear projection. They differ significantly in their characteristics, affecting both the appropriate size of viewing area and the tolerable level of ambient lighting.

Types of front projection screens

For front projection, four types of opaque reflective screen are in common use:

- Matte screens, which have non-glossy, non-directional surfaces that appear to have essentially the same brightness from all points within the viewing area, and hence a relatively wide viewing angle. In addition to the flexible variety, fiberboard or plaster walls, finished with a flat white paint may serve as matte screens, although they will lack brilliance.

- Beaded screens, which have white surfaces coated with fine glass beads that reflect light toward its source. This produces a bright image over a rather small maximum viewing angle.

- Lenticular screens, whose surfaces have very small parallel lens-like serrations that serve to control light reflectance so as to produce maximum brightness over a specified maximum viewing angle. Some types provide a uniformly bright image over an area comparable to that provided by a matte screen.

- Metallized screens, which are coated with paint having a metallic pigment. These screens may be highly directional, resembling the beaded screens, or their characteristics may be more like those of matte screens. The more specular ones may have undesirable "hot spots" due to reflection.

Rear projection screens

Rear projection screens are necessarily translucent. They serve to accept incident illumination from the projector, and to diffuse and re-radiate it as a visible image. They may be either flexible or rigid, and in both cases, have a roughened surface similar to ground glass to provide diffusion. A variety of screens with widely differing characteristics are available.

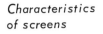

Characteristics of screens

With either projection method, each type of screen has its unique properties. It is essential that the appropriate type be chosen in each situation, and to aid in making a selection, some knowledge of screen characteristics is needed. The more important of these characteristics are identified and defined in the following paragraphs, with brief summary explanations of their effect on the projection system. Unless otherwise stated, these characteristics pertain to front and rear projection screens alike.

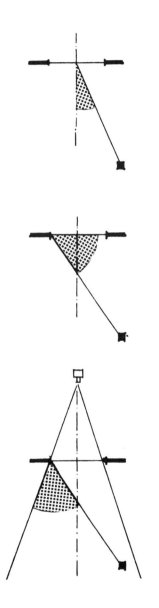

Viewing Angle: The angle used in referring to and evaluating screen characteristics as observed at different locations in the viewing area. It is defined as the angle described at the center of the screen, by the viewer's sight line and the projection axis. Excessive viewing angles will result in reduced brightness or distortion. The maximum viewing angle at which distortion becomes objectionable is about 50°. The maximum viewing angle limited by brightness and contrast will vary with screen and projector and may be as narrow as 20°.

Edge Angle: The angle defined by the surface of the screen and a line from the viewer to the far edge of the screen. Too narrow edge angles will result in distortion and inadequate image brightness. (Either edge angle or viewing angle can be used to define the sides of an appropriate viewing area; in these reports, the former method is used.)

Bend Angle: Another reference angle used in evaluating rear projection screens. It is the angle described by the outermost light ray of the projector and the sight line of any viewer. The maximum bend angle is that angle beyond which the amount of light reaching the viewer is inadequate and will not produce an acceptable image. A limited number of rear projection screens available today are capable of achieving satisfactory images with bend angles in excess of 50°. (This angle is also critical in determining the maximum width of the seating area).

Screen Brightness: This is the measure, in foot lamberts, of the light intensity observed on the screen—reflected light on a front projection screen and luminous intensity on a rear projection screen. Brightness is independent of viewing distance, but varies with the viewing angle. It is fundamental to the production of a good image. Without adequate brightness, color, contrast and detail are lost. It is also a critical factor in establishing the permissible level of room lighting during projection. Screen brightness is determined by the light output of the projector, the size of the image, and the reflecting or transmitting properties of the screen itself. A small image will have four times the screen brightness of an image of doubled dimensions (quadrupled area) produced by the same projector at twice the throw distance. Thus, to retain acceptable brightness, other factors remaining constant, the larger the image desired, the more powerful the projector required.

In small spaces the brightness of a 2- or 3-foot image, even with front projection (and an appropriate screen) may be sufficiently high to be clearly seen under subdued daylight, but in larger spaces requiring larger images, adequate brightness is obtainable economically only by rear projection. This is because a front projection screen is designed to reflect all light including ambient light, and the reflection of room ambient light increases the non-image brightness thereby reducing contrast. A rear projection screen may reflect as little as 5% of the ambient light striking it, thus greatly increasing contrast and clarity of image.

Several authorities have recommended appropriate screen brightness levels for various projected media. Most of these recommendations, however, are based on darkened room conditions, whereas in educational applications, the provision of some room lighting is essential. Consequently, the authors feel that because of certain important differences, the professional standards are not necessarily always applicable to educational requirements. As the result of considerable experience with educational projected media, and a comprehensive study of screen characteristics, it is recommended that for practical purposes, the minimum acceptable brightness of screens for school use should be 5 Ft. L. when films or slides are shown, and not less than 2 Ft. L. for projected TV. (See "Standards") It should be emphasized that the lowest values are marginal values and apply to the poorest seat in the viewing area. All other seats will have better viewing. Higher values are, of course, desirable if economically feasible.

Brightness Ratio: The ratio between the maximum and minimum screen brightness, at different parts of the screen, as seen from a given observation point. The theoretically ideal ratio would be 1:1, but actually, variations within a certain range are not detectable by the normal observer. A ratio of 2 or 3 to 1 is very good. As the ratio increases to 10:1, observers will readily detect "hot spots".

Image Brightness: Screen brightness measured in Ft. L. with the projector operating to project light only, with no slide or film in the aperature (see Contrast Ratio).

Non-Image Brightness: Screen brightness measured with the projector operating, but with the lens capped, and with room lighting at the level normally used during projection images. It is measured in foot lamberts (see Contrast Ratio).

Contrast Ratio: The ratio of image brightness to non-image brightness, as seen from any given observation point. (It differs for almost every position in the viewing area). Since non-image brightness determines how black the darkest portion of the image can be, Contrast Ratio is the relationship between the lightest possible portion to the darkest possible portion of the image.

Ambient room light falling on the screen affects image contrast, and the maximum contrast ratio obtainable is largely determined by the level of lighting desired in the room. To obtain adequate task lighting and at the same time a high contrast ratio requires a correspondingly high level of screen brightness. With less-than-adequate projector output, either the level of ambient light striking the screen must be reduced or a lower contrast ratio must be accepted.

The desirable contrast ratio varies with the type of material being shown. It can be relatively low (5:1) for black-and-white line drawings, but should be much higher (as high as 100:1) for color having a range of intermediate values. A ratio of 30:1 is marginal for color material.

Screen Gain: The ratio between the observed brightness of the screen at any point on the screen, and its actual illumination (by the projector) at that point. Its measured value always varies with the viewing angle, and is determined in different ways for front and rear projection screens. For front projection screens, screen gain is defined as the ratio between the intensity of light reflected by the screen from the projector, and that reflected from the same point by a pure magnesium carbonate target. For rear projection screens, it is simply the ratio between the brightness on the viewer's side of the screen (measured in Foot-Lamberts) and the incident illumination at the same point on the projector side (measured in Foot-Candles).

$$\text{Gain} = \frac{\text{output (Ft. L.)}}{\text{input (Ft. C.)}}$$

Since the screen is a passive element, it can, of course, produce no overall net gain; gains in some areas are offset by compensating losses in others. There is actually, in fact, an overall loss, varying with the light transmission or reflectance efficiency of the screen, which is never 100%.

Gain characteristics of screens are always of prime importance, because gain largely determines the quality of image in respect to viewer location. Screens referred to as high gain screens concentrate the light output of the projector along a very limited cone, thus restricting viewing angles and areas but permitting a high level of ambient light. Low gain screens diffuse light across a wider cone, but suffer a corresponding loss of brightness and produce images with less contrast tolerating less ambient light.

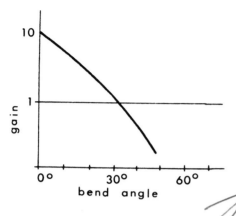

gain

10

1

0°   30°   60°

bend angle

<u>Gain Curve</u>: A graph representing the screen gain over a range of viewing angles.

Beaded screens which have the highest gain factor of any of the front projection types have a correspondingly low maximum viewing angle of about 20°. Matte screens, on the other hand, have lower, but much more uniform gain characteristics, with a wider viewing angle; lenticular screens can be designed for a range of viewing angles. The gain characteristics of rear projection screens vary a good deal, and the range of their maximum viewing angles is generally greater than those of the front projection screens.

An ideal screen would have a gain of about 3 to a bend angle of 60° and then fall off sharply.

<u>Screen Reflection Factor</u>: This is a term used in reference to rear projection screens to identify the proportion of ambient light falling on the screen that is reflected by the screen to an observer. The lower this factor, the better will be the contrast ratio (and image clarity) at a given ambient light level.

The reflection factor is an important consideration in all learning spaces where room lighting level is to be suitable for note-taking. The lower this factor is, the higher can be the ambient light without seriously affecting the image. A screen reflection factor of 5% would be ideal, but factors as high as 35% must occasionally be tolerated in order to obtain sufficiently high gain values at bend angles in excess of 50°. A low factor is obviously undesirable on a front projection screen, because high reflectivity is the basic requirement of such screens. With the rapid improvements being made in screen design, however, it seems likely that screen brightness (and contrast) may be improved to such an extent that the reflection of ambient light may be much less critical, at least in the smaller screen sizes.

All of these characteristics should be considered in determining the appropriate type of screen for a given situation. Obviously, they are inter-related, and the relative importance of each depends on many factors, not the least of which is the type of material being shown.

Interrelationships among these characteristics

If only black-and-white line drawings were to be projected, or if a screen were to be used exclusively for showing 16mm color travel-ogue movies, or used only for TV projection, optimum values for the various characteristics could be established. But in the learning spaces, such specific and exclusive uses will rarely if ever be en-countered. Instead, the screens in these spaces normally serve for projecting the widest possible range of material. Consequently, and also because of wide variations in other critical factors, the selection of the right screen necessarily involves the weighing of advantages and disadvantages, and intelligent compromise. In most cases, the most important considerations are screen gain, contrast ratio, and the maximum viewing angle over which a clear image can be easily seen.

PROJECTORS

A caution

The reader is cautioned that any discussion of projection devices can only report on the existing ranges and characteristics of commercially available equipment. Technological developments can render much of today's equipment obsolete; at the time equipment is selected, the newest models should be investigated for improvements in optical systems, lumen output, remote capability, ease of operation, and cost.

Overhead projector

The overhead projector currently is one of the most popular projection devices in classrooms. Ease and speed of transparency-making, high lumen output, elimination of the need for room darkening and ease of operation are among its good characteristics. The only special requirement for this projector is a tilted screen in order to prevent keystoning of the image. Projectors range from fanless desktop models to those which include the projection of slides and filmstrip through the projector's optical system. Prices range from $150 to $1000, and lamp wattages are available from 300 to 1000 watts.

35mm slide projector

The classroom use of 35mm color slides has substantially increased with the production of inexpensive, foolproof 35mm cameras and remotely controlled projectors. With the low cost of slide production and the space savings in storage, the 35mm slide is being used more and more extensively than the 3-¼'' x 4'' slide. For efficient use in classrooms, the projectors should be capable of remote on-off, forward-reverse, and focus. Ideally, the fan should have a thermal device to allow cooling of the projector after the lamp is turned off. Highly desirable characteristics for a projector will be ease of loading, low cost of slide trays that accept all sorts of mountings, and freedom from jamming. Lenses are available that will allow projection from as short a distance as 1W (1 width of the screen) for rear projection to 6W for front projection in larger auditoriums. With improvements in lumen output, mirrors can be used to reduce the space required for rear screen projection. Projectors are available with xenon light sources, random access, digital readout and audio projector programming. Lamp wattage ranges from 300 to 1200 watts and prices range from $100 to $6000.

3-¼" x 4" slide projector

Most 3-¼" x 4" slide projectors manufactured today are of the manually operated type. For the purpose of this report and where remote control of the projection device is necessary, the few remotely operated projectors currently available are discussed. Some of the most desirable characteristics of these projectors are high lumen output, the capability with an adapter of projecting 35mm slides, the ability to handle polaroid slides, and short-throw lenses for rear screen projection. Prices for the remote-controlled projectors range from $1500 to over $3000 with wattages of 3000 and more.

Motion picture projectors

Currently the 16mm projector has a monopoly on motion picture projection in the classroom. However, with the introduction of the new, large frame 8mm film and sound cameras, there may be a marked change-over to 8mm for small group use and it will be introduced for independent study. Film projection using 35mm film has never found extensive educational application.

It is desirable for optimum use that the motion picture projectors be remotely controlled for on-off, stop frame and focus. Also, some method must be devised to prevent film burns when the projector lamp is turned off, such as delay on the fan circuit or a thermal delay. Industry is trying to make it easier to thread motion picture projectors; perhaps the most promising development is that of the film cartridge-loaded projector. In order to use a motion picture projector for rear screen projection, the image must be reversed. This may be handled using a tank prism, a mirror (first surface if close to the projector), or a lens with an internal mirror or prism. In general, the smaller the aperture, the more lumen output required to obtain a specified image brightness. However, high lumen output can, in time, effect the color dyes of the films. Lenses are available for throw distances of 1-½W and greater.

Film strip projectors and previewers

The low cost and availability of film strips on almost every subject makes this form of visual aid attractive to many teachers. Projectors

with remote control are required for rear screen projection. Simple film strip previewers may adequately serve the student studying independently. In between, are projectors appropriate for front projection with small groups. Projectors vary in price from $60 to $300 and previewers from $15 to $30. Lamp wattage range from 150 to 1200 watts.

Television projectors

Television projection has its greatest implications for large group instruction. Its use as a method of displaying and magnifying gross images is excellent. Its promise as a first rate teaching tool is dependent, not only on its ability to have good contrast, brightness and definition, but also simple maintenance. Projectors are available for closed circuit or broadcast in either black and white or color and black and white. In general, the more expensive the projector, the more acceptable the image and the higher the lumen output. Projected television requires slightly more than a 2W throw distance. Prices vary tremendously from $2800 to $50,000 or so.

More information

For more comprehensive information on projection equipment the reader is directed to the Audio-visual Equipment Directory, National Audio-Visual Association, Inc., 1201 Spring Street, Fairfax, Virginia.

Space for rear projection

In designing for rear projection, one of the problems the architect faces is the allowance of the correct amount of space for the location of the projection equipment. Figure 1 shows a projector located at a 1W throw distance and indicates the maximum bend angle for seat A as over 75°. This is unsatisfactory for this seat; the allowable bend angle is established by the screen characteristics, and at present, the maximum bend angle is 60°. Figure 2 shows a 2W throw distance and a maximum bend angle at seat A of about 60° which is satisfactory. Figure 3 shows a total depth of rear projection area as 1W, but by using a mirror, still permits a 2W throw distance and a 60° bend angle.

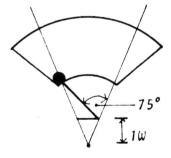

FIGURE 1

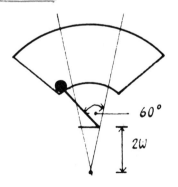

FIGURE 2

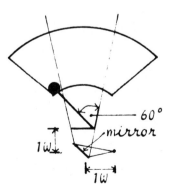

FIGURE 3

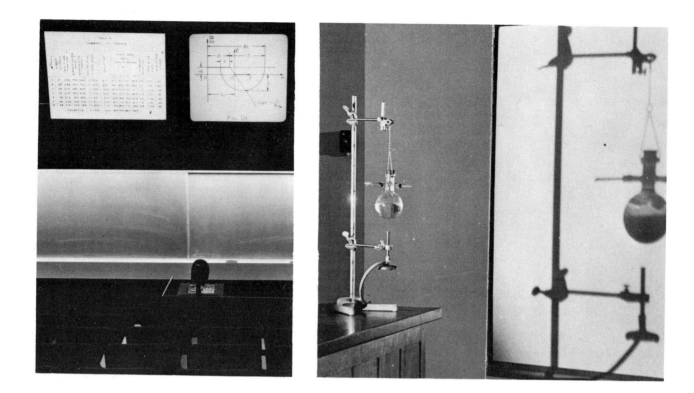

Mirrors reduce light

The use of mirrors, however, has its drawback in that about a 10% loss of image brightness occurs. One must also be careful of reflections of ambient light of other projectors or classroom light passing through other screens and affecting either the mirror or the screen. This can be combatted by locating black drapes to mask the projectors from this stray light.

Some general rules

A few general rules are helpful in locating projectors and establishing space for rear projection equipment:

- the larger the screen, the longer the throw distance, and conversely,

- the smaller the screen, the shorter the throw distance.

- mirrors may be used to fold the projection beam for space saving with smaller screens or with projectors with high lumen output on larger screens.

- for initial schematic design a 2W depth behind all the screens should be allocated for the rear projection area.

- the use of extra close-up lenses decreases the viewing area, and may result in some distortion around the edge of projected images.

CONTROLS

*Most projection
equipment
remote controlled*

Wherever projected media are used, the instructor should be in complete control of the presentation. With rear projection, this necessarily requires remote control. Except in small seminar and conference situations, front projection should also be remotely controlled by the instructor, whether the projector is located in a permanent booth or within the learning space itself. In most cases, several projectors will be used and the instructor, from his lectern or station, should be able to call upon any of them at will. All of the material to be projected must be selected beforehand, arranged in proper sequence and positioned in the projectors. In the smaller spaces, this will probably be the instructor's own responsibility; in the larger spaces, the material will likely be turned over to a technician responsible for loading and servicing the projectors.

*Light automatically
controlled with
projectors*

The instructor should also have control of room lighting. This does not mean that the choice of proper lighting levels should be his, but that he should control the change from one predetermined level to another, as the presented media requires. In small spaces this will be done by properly located wall switches, but in other rooms the lighting level should be automatically set at the appropriate predetermined level for each media and controlled by the projector switches. Thus, lighting is controlled by the instructor, but he does not choose the level of lighting used during projection.

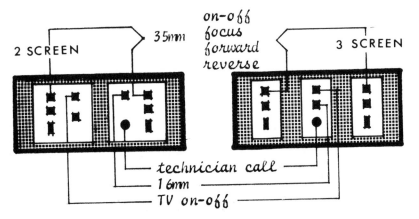

*Design of the
control panel*

The diagram illustrates control panels for the use of two or three screens. Note that although these switches do control room lighting, they are not identified as lighting controls. The appropriate levels of lighting are provided automatically as the various projectors are activated, and when no projectors are running, room lighting automatically returns to the "working" level. The controls should be grouped on the panel to correspond to screen positions. For rear projection, or for front projection from a permanent booth, a 3" conduit should be provided between the instructor's station and the projection area to accommodate the necessary wiring.

PROJECTED MATERIAL

*Classes of
projected material*

The Eastman Kodak Company classifies projected material as follows:

Class A: Full-scale continuous-tone black-and-white or color pictures in which pictorial values are important and color or tone differences must be discriminated. Minimum contrast ratio—100:1

Class B: Color diagrams and continuous-tone black-and-white pictures in high key. Minimum contrast ratio—25:1

Class C: Simple line material, such as text, tables, diagrams and graphs, either positive or negative. Minimum contrast ratio—5:1

*Importance of
legibility
standards*

Because the contrast requirement for Class C material is relatively low, the importance of the legibility of such material is sometimes overlooked in its preparation, but it is critical. Any projection material containing letters, numerals, or other symbols should be prepared with legibility uppermost in mind. Certain standards have been developed to insure ready perception; if H is the height of the image, than the smallest lettering should be no less than H/50, typical lettering should be H/40 and title lettering H/20.

THE VIEWING AREA

*Viewing area
not critical
in most classrooms*

Before projected materials were introduced, the objects to be viewed in the usual schoolroom were the instructor, the chalkboards, and sometimes maps and charts. The instructor was free to move about the room, and the other objects of visual attention were usually distributed over several wall areas. All of them received their illumination by the general lighting of the room itself. With no fixed area of attention, sightlines and viewing were not critical, as long as the general lighting was adequate.

*Projected images
restrict viewing area*

For the effective use of visual aids, however, the requirements for good viewing are much more demanding. The projected image necessarily occupies a fixed position, and, except on the TV receiver, is in a flat plane. Whereas a three-dimensional object may well be viewed from the side, a flat picture can be seen intelligibly only within the limits of a "cone of view". To see the image properly, the viewer must be within the limits of this cone, and neither too near the image nor too far from it. The area defined by these limits is referred to as the viewing area. Its importance in the planning of spaces for image viewing is fundamental, whether the space be a small informal conference area or a large formal lecture hall.

Shape of the viewing area

The shape of the viewing area, then, is approximately as shown. Its size is always based on the size of the image to be viewed. The human eye comprehends detail only within a limited cone angle (about 2-½ minutes of arc), and the length of chord subtending this arc, e.g. the image width, varies with its distance from the observer. Thus an object 20 feet away and 6 feet long appears the same as a similar object 10 feet away and 3 feet long. The size of the viewing area is determined by three dimensions:

- The Minimum Distance, (1), which is the distance from the nearest part of the image to the eye of the closest viewer,

- The Maximum Distance, (2), which is the distance from the furthermost part of the image to the most distant viewer, and

- The Maximum Viewing Angle, (3), which is the angle between the projection axis and the line of sight of a person located as far from this axis as he can be and still see all image detail in proper brilliance.

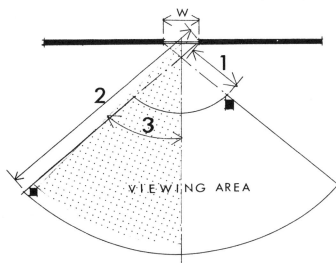

VIEWING AREA

Two ways of establishing the viewing angle

Whether the apex of the Maximum Viewing Angle should be located at the screen or at some other point on the projection axis is a moot point. There is some disagreement among authorities, too, as to how it should govern the side limits of the viewing area. Some prefer the use of the "edge angle", while others use the angle at the center of the screen. By either approach, the limits defined are essentially similar. In this study, an edge angle of 40° has been used in laying out viewing areas for rear projection, since it is felt this best represents average screen characteristics. With front projection, the use of the "center angle" is probably more common practice, and its values range from 20° to possibly as high as 50°, again depending on factors which were explained in the discussion of screens. The maximum value of the angle used in determining the viewing area for receiver TV is 45°.

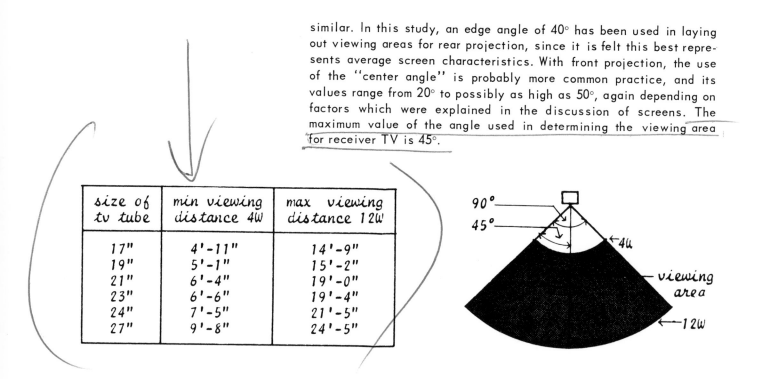

size of tv tube	min viewing distance 4W	max viewing distance 12W
17"	4'-11"	14'-9"
19"	5'-1"	15'-2"
21"	6'-4"	19'-0"
23"	6'-6"	19'-4"
24"	7'-5"	21'-5"
27"	9'-8"	24'-5"

Defining minimum and maximum viewing distances

Practical minimum and maximum distances are both expressed as multiples of the image width (W). They vary both with the medium being used and with the type and quality of material being projected, and may be affected also, in some degree, by personal preferences. They have not yet been precisely determined by scientific methods, and it's doubtful that such data would have much practical value anyway. The generally accepted values, resulting from numerous studies, are these:

	Film, Slides and projected TV	TV Receivers
Minimum distance	2 W	4 W
Maximum distance	6 W to 10 W	12 W

Relation of screen size and viewing area

Since the size of the viewing area is a function of the image width, it follows that the proper screen size for any given space will be determined by the number of viewers intended. Conversely, a given type and size of screen automatically establishes the size of the viewing area, and consequently the size of audience that can be properly accommodated. The viewing area is the pattern which determines the seating arrangement in any learning space where projected images are to be effectively used, and in the larger spaces, at least, it also influences the shape of the room.

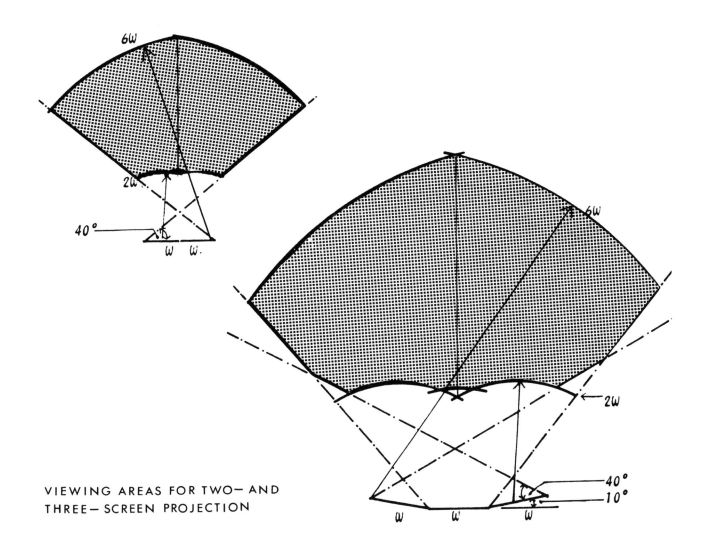

VIEWING AREAS FOR TWO— AND THREE— SCREEN PROJECTION

PLANNING THE PROJECTION SYSTEM

Steps in design

Whether front or rear projection is to be used, the design of the projection system itself involves determining:

a) the size of viewing area required

b) the appropriate screen size

c) the proper type of screen

d) the appropriate projector(s)—the required lumen output, focal length and location

e) the maximum permissible level of ambient lighting on the screen.

*Trial and
error at first*

The desired audience size is usually predetermined. In some cases, the size of the viewing area, too, may be established by existing conditions. Otherwise, its size and shape should be tentatively approximated in accord with the principles already discussed. Because of the relationship between its dimensions and the width of screen to be used, the inexperienced designer necessarily proceeds by trail and error, until he arrives at a satisfactory arrangement accommodating the specified audience in proper relationship with the screen. Sometimes, the problem may be reversed, requiring a determination of the optimum audience and seating arrangement for projection equipment already at hand.

Several helpful brochures and articles have been published which explain in detail the selection of components for projection systems. Among these are

- Space for Audio-Visual Large Group Instruction, University Facilities Research Center, Madison Wisconsin 1963

- Foundation for Effective Audio-Visual Projection, Eastman Kodak Co., 1957

- Components for Rear Projection Systems, School of Architecture, Rensselaer Polytechnic Institute, Troy, N.Y. 1964

- "Effects of Stray Light on the Quality of Projected Pictures at Various Levels of Screen Brightness"; Raymond L. Estes; Journal of the SMPTE; 1953

- "Selection and Specification of Rear-Projection Screens"; Petro Vlahos; Journal of the SMPTE; 1961.

- "Operational Characteristics of Rear Projection;" John F. Dreyer; Journal of the SMPTE; 1959

STANDARDS

Professional standards accepted by the Society of Motion Picture and Television Engineers have been developed for viewing front and rear projected images. These standards provide excellent images. However, for the purpose of economy in classroom use of projected media, it is felt that some standards based on the poorest seat in the room can be lowered, particularly for gross images. The following resume of standards indicates by asterisk (*) those that are less than the professional standards.

Screen Brightness

Motion Pictures:

    5 Ft.L. - Minimum* (gross images)
   10 Ft.L. - Satisfactory
   15 Ft.L. - Excellent
   20 Ft.L. - Maximum (flicker threshold for some observers)

Slides:

    2.5 Ft.L. - Minimum* (gross images)
      5 Ft.L. - Minimum for slides with detail
     10 Ft.L. - Satisfactory
     20 Ft.L. - Excellent

Projected TV:

    2 Ft.L. - Minimum* (gross images)
   20 Ft.L. - Maximum (flicker threshold for some observers)

TV Monitors:

    100 lumens per square foot

Brightness Ratio

    2:1 - Excellent
    3:1 - Very good
   10:1 - Acceptable* under some conditions

Contrast Ratio

   100:1 - Pictorial scenes
    25:1 - Good legibility of printed characters
     5:1 - White letters on black background
    30:1 - Minimum* contrast ratio for poorest seat dictated by higher levels of classroom light and many types of projected materials.

Contrast ratio is determined in part by non-image brightness which, in turn, is related to screen reflectance and room ambient light. Therefore, controlling the amount of ambient light reaching the screen is important. For large screen installations, if the amount of ambient light occuring at the screen is held to 1-2 Ft.C., the contrast ratio will normally be adequate.

Writing Surface Lighting Levels

Ideally, an average ratio of 1:1 between writing surface brightness and screen brightness should be maintained, while not spilling excessive ambient light on the screens. Since screen brightness varies for each seat in the viewing area, the average condition of brightness for each broad class of projected material should be approximately satisfied. For a medium to large size room, three lighting levels would be in the range of:

    5-10 Ft.C. - Projected TV and films
   10-20 Ft.C. - Slides
   30 + Ft.C. - Other class activities

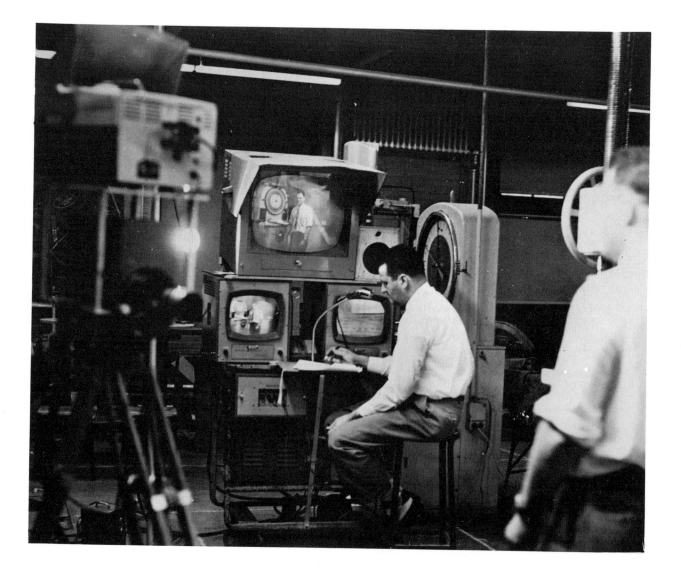

5 HARDWARE FOR MEDIA: OTHER EQUIPMENT

Hardware as a panacea

For many years, the educational market was not considered significant by the audio-visual industry; schools had little money for hardware, and what equipment they purchased was developed primarily for home, industry or government use. With the passage of the National Defense Education Act and other governmental and foundation support, industry recognized a vast, new market; the race to produce educational hardware began and educators were engulfed by salesmen whose products were the answer to all their needs. The acquisition of hardware became a status symbol, but unfortunately too little time was spent in planning its incorporation into a total system supporting specified educational objectives. The problem is still with us; the following review of additional available hardware is offered to indicate some of the potential available to education, but which must be employed within the context of purpose and need. Even so, much of what is mentioned will soon be obsoleted by newer, more desirable hardware.

Wet and dry carrels

Current interest in independent study and programmed instruction has introduced a new line of hardware—independent study is often housed in a study carrel, for which there are no standards as to size, shape or location. At present, carrels are designated as either "dry" or "wet". A "dry" carrel will provide writing surface, semi-isolation and storage, and depending upon its location and use, may also provide task surface lighting and an electrical outlet for portable projection and recording devices or teaching machines. The "wet" carrel introduces audio and video into an acoustically treated or totally private carrel. This requires that the designer provide conduit to the carrel from a distribution center.

Teaching machines

The teaching machine is a vehicle for programmed materials and is generally used in an independent study situation. The size, shape and complexity of these devices vary greatly; the more complicated

ones may use both projected images and audio, while others may merely require the student to view written information and answer multiple choice questions. They are usually portable and may be used on the classroom desk or at a study carrel. The designer is only concerned when these devices need electric or electronic connections; for the most part only 110V AC power is required.

Student response systems

A student response system allows a teacher to immediately evaluate the effectiveness of his presentation. Each student station is equipped with a response unit of 4 or 5 buttons, and a correct answer indicator. The teacher's console contains indicators or meters corresponding to each response button. The teacher poses a multiple choice question and the student presses the button corresponding to what he believes is the correct answer. The instructor can see immediately the percentage of responses to each choice. A record of answers for each student can be made on punched tape or stored in a computer, while the student immediately receives visual display of the correct answer. Of the many response systems available today, most all require wiring from the student station to the teacher's console and power unit. In order to plan for such a system, it is necessary to know the number and location of the student stations and to provide conduit which is accessible at the appropriate locations.

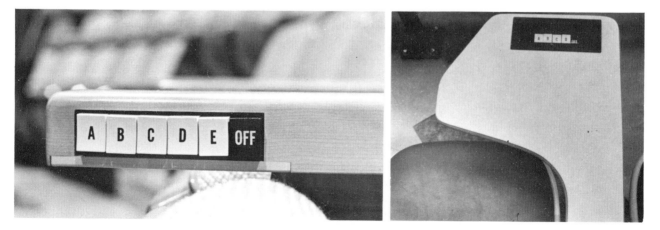

Traditional display surfaces

The most traditional display surface is the chalkboard, but the black slate surface of the past has now changed to a porcelainized steel surface available in a variety of colors. For displaying prepared visuals, an easel holding sequential charts, a flannel board, or magnetic board may be used. The flannel board is covered with chemically treated flannel. Anything to be displayed on this surface is backed with a nylon material that will adhere to the flannel even when lightly placed against it. The magnetic board, which may double as a chalkboard, holds charts by magnetic attractors. In addition, classrooms will have some tackboard surfaces which are available in many colors and which can be attached to any surface.

Television monitors and receivers

The use of television as a teaching tool has increased greatly since the mid-1950's and with technological improvements and price decreases, it seems destined to be come a standard aid in tomorrow's school. Both monitors and receivers are presently used in schools for reception. A monitor is a high definition set without tuner or audio that is connected directly to a TV camera or to a closed circuit system. A receiver is similar to a home TV set and may be tuned to various closed circuit channels or to off-the-air programs. The introduction of monitors or receivers into the average classroom does not pose special problems for the designer, as long as they are positioned to cover all seats with adequate viewing. However, when they are to be located in a large group instruction room where other media will be used, they require careful placement to avoid interference with other images. When receivers are used, the audio system within the set may be employed for all audio distribution in the room. Monitors will require a separate audio system. There are a number of devices available for hanging the sets from the ceiling or mounting on walls.

Classroom TV systems

The simplest of TV systems is the television camera hooked up directly with monitors, receivers, or a TV projector. This system may be used in a classroom for magnification; a TV camera is located over the lectern slightly above the teacher's head and, by using a zoom lens and auxiliary lighting, graphics, book materials, specimens and small models, may be shown to the entire class. The only requirement for such an internal system is cabling from the camera to the TV receivers and monitors, or to the projector and power outlets. When additional cameras are added, it becomes necessary to add switching devices, which may be portable and located in the classroom, or switching can be controlled remotely.

An "in-house" TV system

If TV originates from an "in-house" studio, distribution will be by coaxial cable to the various classrooms from a control and distribution center. The control center will also contain video tape recorders and film and slide chains. Because of rapid equipment advances, cabling between the studio, studio control and distribution

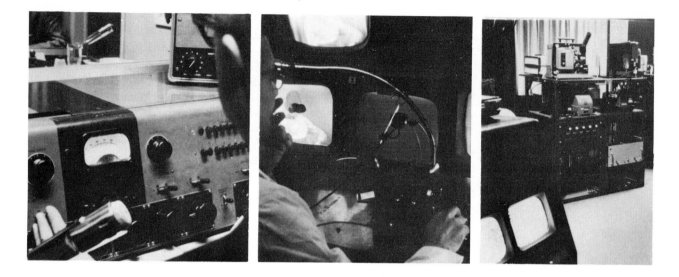

center should be easily accessible. This may be done by using an elevated floor in these areas or by the use of open cable trays.

Video tape recorders

The importance of Video Tape Recording should not be underestimated, and as the price of the VTR decreases, its use will become more important. Effective educational television today is hampered by the necessity to schedule all classes for simultaneous presentation. VTR's can allow schools to schedule individually to best fit their programs. The use of educational TV stations during off-hours for broadcasting courses to be taped at the schools will make many more hours of special courses available, especially in rural areas.

Television distribution

From a central origination and distribution point, television signals may be carried to viewers or recorders in schools and institutions by several means. Closed circuit systems employing coaxial cable or telephone lines may be extended between buildings. In addition, standard micro-wave and 2500 megacycle transmission may be used from point to point. By employing translators their range may be extended. Of course, conventional, multi-directional broadcast television may also be used. Reception of TV signals at the school requires a receiver antenna carefully oriented for effective reception.

Audio laboratories

The audio laboratory, formerly known as the language laboratory, is composed of student stations each with audio listening and recording capability, a teacher's console with monitoring capability, and tape storage, recording and playback. There are many different laboratories available, each with its own merits and limitations. As a general rule, the student stations are placed in rows and conduit is run from the teacher's console or tape decks to a floor box at the end of each row. At the console 110-120V 60 cycle, AC current is required.

Computers

Previously, the potential of the computer coupled with a student response system for research and analysis purposes was suggested. Some other uses of the computer are as a teaching machine using a branching program, as an information storage and retrieval system, and as an administrative tool for scheduling, record keeping, payroll, and the like. It is impossible to offer general suggestions for planning an efficient computer system since each installation must meet unique local requirements. Computer modules should be placed on a raised floor, the computer room should have a strictly controlled environment, and be relatively dust-free and acoustically treated.

Classroom communication systems

Finally, the architect should be familiar with the combination communications systems that are available for school plants. From a number of origination points, audio and video information may be fed to classrooms, and, in turn, information may be carried between classrooms and from classrooms to offices, studios and so on. Each classroom is equipped with a panel which may contain clock, telephone, intercom, microphone and television jack, light controls, thermostat, emergency call, and the controls for television receivers used within the room. Such a multi-communications system can be built initially, while components may be added as functional usage increases.

THE CENTER FOR ARCHITECTURAL RESEARCH
RENSSELAER POLYTECHNIC INSTITUTE

Rensselaer's Center for Architectural Research was established in the fall of 1965 as a department within the School of Architecture. The establishment of the Center formalized a program of architectural research which had been developing over a period of some ten years.

The Center has three main objectives: offering problem-solving services for foundation, governmental, and industrial sponsors; assisting the architectural profession and building industry through the dissemination of information resulting from research efforts; and strengthening architectural education at Rensselaer through the development of graduate programs based on architectural research, and offering of research options to undergraduates.

DEPARTMENT OF AUDIOVISUAL INSTRUCTION
NATIONAL EDUCATION ASSOCIATION

The Department of Audiovisual Instruction of the National Education Association is made up of 6,500 individuals who are concerned with the improvement of instruction through the application of educational technology —that branch of educational theory and practice concerned primarily with the design and use of messages which control the learning process. DAVI members include teachers, librarians, audiovisual directors, research workers, and communication specialists.

Members receive the monthly magazine, *Audiovisual Instruction*, and the quarterly journal, *AV Communication Review*, as well as regular service packet mailings. Other activities include the annual convention, an active national committee program, workshops, plus consultation and placement services. Write for more information and a publications list: DAVI, 1201 Sixteenth Street, N.W., Washington, D.C. 20036.